I'M NOT REALLY HERE

Also by Tim Allen

Don't Stand Too Close to a Naked Man

I'M NOT REALLY HERE

TIM ALLEN

NEW YORK

None of what I do happens without the love and laughter
given so freely by my dear wife and daughter,
and the absolute magic, strength, and love in life
which I humbly refer to as God.

SPECIAL THANKS

This difficult, challenging, and often mind-bending project was, in no small part, accomplished due to the hard work and many talents of my friend David Rensin. Together we sought truth, enlightenment, and the quantum punchline. He was good company.

*

Many thanks also to Kim Flagg and Chris Rush, two very bright stars from whom I continually gathered light.

Credit is also due the vast world-wide Internet, without which it would have been impossible to finish the research and work on the book while shooting a film in the rain forest.

Finally, I am indebted to the many scientific and spiritual explorers whose groundbreaking ideas preceded and inspired me — especially Robert Pirsig, whose classic book, *Zen and the Art of Motorcycle Maintenance*, started me on this road to self-discovery so many years ago.

"No one, not one person, has ever seen an atom."
— Gary Zukav, *The Dancing Wu Li Masters*

"The world of matter is a relative world, and an illusory one: illusory not in the sense that it does not exist, but illusory in the sense that we do not see it as it really is."
— Gary Zukav, *The Dancing Wu Li Masters*

"What guarantee is there that the five senses, taken together, do cover the whole of possible experience? . . . There are gaps between the fingers; there are gaps between the senses. In these gaps is the darkness which hides the connection between things . . . The darkness is the source of our vague fears and anxieties, but also the home of the Gods."
— Alan Watts, *The Book*

I'M
NOT
REALLY
HERE

THE DREAM IS always the same . . .

I'm deep in the Venezuelan jungle. My helicopter touches down on top of a huge rock plateau. I jump out and get busy unloading supplies, when suddenly what seems like a beautiful day turns black, and the biggest storm I have ever seen appears out of nowhere. Thunder, lightning, wild winds, and sheets of rain attack the area. I run for cover and signal to the pilot to get the hell off the plateau and make for clear skies, otherwise the copter could be damaged and we'd be stuck here forever. As he rises and disappears into the distance, I realize that there's nothing for me to do but find a place to wait while the storm exhausts itself.

It's a long wait. The air's grown colder, the sky darker. The tempest is unrelenting. This means the chopper might not be back until daybreak. I've been hunkering under a stone outcropping, trying to stay dry, but what I really need is to find somewhere safe to sleep.

I'm just about to cross a clearing and search for shelter when the clouds part for an instant and a searing beam of sunlight strikes a rock wall about twenty yards away. On the face appears to be an opening. Unless the wind and water, over the centuries, can carve a *perfect oval*, it is definitely man made.

An inner voice tells me to enter and get out of the storm.

Another inner voice warns me off.

"Don't go in there, you idiot! Remember the movie, 'Friday the 13th'?"

A third inner voice tries to give me a hard time for not listening to my wife when she said I should forget about going to the jungle and take my family to Disneyworld instead.

"Shut up, all of you," I say. "Who can make a decision with everyone talking at once? I'm going in." I may sound brave but I have no choice.

This is the scary part. I step through the ancient aperture and feel the smooth rock walls brush my shoulders. Once inside, I click on my Durabeam survival flashlight and see that the immediate area is choked with debris. A closer look reveals that it's a pile of human bones. And tiny pieces of brightly colored foil. The fate of these poor souls scares me too much to try and figure out the connection. In fact, I'm so shook up that my flashlight slips from my sweaty hand into a pile of skulls. Now I have to root around to find it. Yuck! Fortunately the unit turns on immediately and I take a moment to thank the gods of impact-resistance for their strict manufacturing requirements.

I know I can't stay here, so I sweep the area with my quite-expensive waterproof beacon, and what I see once again takes my breath away. The small foyer opens into a cavern that is so large that even the halogen beam of my trusty hand-torch cannot find the far wall through the inky blackness.

All of a sudden things begin to make sense.

The local residents, descendants of the Penari Indians, have long thought the Maquamatqu — or, roughly translated, "room of Answers" — is hidden among the billion-year-old rock plateaus, or

Tepui, as they are known to the locals who have long believed them to be home to both gods and devils. Many have searched for the lost room, the most famous being the American bush pilot Freddy Angelo. After countless South American expeditions, Angelo vanished without a trace in the early 1940s.

Somehow I know that my presence here cannot be an accident. I believe that I have been shown the portal as part of a larger purpose. In fact, I am so overcome with the sense that the Room of Answers is nearby that I can literally feel my pulse pounding through my body. As it turns out, my watch band is too tight.

I check the area again with my high-intensity flare. Now that my eyes have adjusted to the dim light, I can see that the cavern floor is in reality a huge underground lake. Either that, or the Penaris never discovered the floor drain. I also see what appear to be steps floating on the surface of the black water. I decide bravely to cross them into the darkness and meet whatever fate awaits me.

Almost immediately I hit a wet spot and nearly fall into the water. Even though I manage to regain my balance, I will remember the moment forever: My $295, guaranteed waterproof-for-life hiking boots are wet, and let me tell you they are NOT waterproof!

That's when I see the structure. It is magnificent. Before me are two pyramids attached apex to apex, rising almost 200 feet. The floating stones lead to a doorway.

Inside is a temple and, well . . . it looks exactly like you'd expect the temple of a lost civilization to look: Raiders of the Lost Ark-ish, oversized, ornate, but cleaner. Not exactly to my taste, and, as I suspected, no floor drain. There are crystals everywhere and gold stuff, and some weird primitive statues that I figure either represent virility and fertility, or are just some guys with hockey sticks attacking two chubby ladies selling watermelons.

On a huge lapis stone set in the center of the enormous main chamber I see an ornate sculpture that looks a lot like a dead tree in a Macy's Christmas window. From the branches hang a dozen bejeweled, egg-shaped ornaments. Each different, but each clearly made by the same hand, and each bearing an insignia that looks like the letters "T" and "A," only made by someone with remedial writing skills. I pluck one and open it. Yes! Within this fabulous gold and jewel-encrusted work of magnificence, written on a tiny stone tablet, is an Answer. I open another. Again, an Answer. How do I know this? I just know. The "T" and "A" markings stand for: The Answer. It's almost impossible to comprehend, but I have found them: The Answers To Everything! The solution to the riddle of the existence and our place in the universe. The answer to the human condition. No longer will we wonder who we are and why we're really here. These ancient eggs harbor the dreams of mankind since mankind began to dream. And, if I'm lucky, a way to consistently pick winning lottery numbers.

There's also a dish of foil-wrapped candies, but I'm too excited to eat.

I quickly open up the other jeweled eggs, then prop my Durabeam on a shelf and sit back to absorb the mysteries of the universe. Darn, not in English! As best as I can figure, the first Answer translates roughly as "Eat your vegetables."

I want to read more, but I'm so exhausted that I just fall asleep where I'm sitting. I do not dream within my dream. No way I can top this one.

The next thing I know, I hear the whirr of chopper blades in the distance, cutting through the thick and humid morning air. I wipe the sleep from my eyes. It's dawn, the storm has let up, and it's time to go. I toss the tiny tablets with the Answers into my backpack. Also, the priceless jeweled eggs, as a little something for the wife. Then I run across the floating stones, through the pile of bones and brightly colored foil, and out onto the Tepui where the helicopter waits.

I suddenly find myself on a plane heading home to America. I realize that the only decent thing to do is to donate this treasure to the Smithsonian Institute. I want to make the tablets available to all mankind, even if mankind has to stand in line to read them. I figure since we've waited this long to evolve, a couple more hours can't hurt.

Before the man from the Smithsonian comes to pick up the tablets, I invite a few close friends over with whom I can share my amazing discovery. We have a fabulous dinner and wonderful conversation, all in anticipation of the main event. Finally, I suggest they go into the library, while I bring in the tablets containing the Answers. I excuse myself and am halfway across the house, thinking that this is the greatest moment of my life, when I suddenly realize — and I know this is going to sound really, really stupid — that I have completely forgotten where I've put the tablets . . .

SATURDAY

ONE

MY EYES SNAP OPEN and I wake
up in the dark. Floating stones, hidden rooms, jeweled eggs, life's
answers, what a dream! Too bad it's not that simple. However, it's
still better than my other recurring dream in which I am naked at
the high school assembly.

The clock reads 3:45 a.m. Great. Now I'll have to spend the
next two hours trying to get back to sleep. It probably won't work.
Strange dreams aside, I've had lots of trouble sleeping lately. Maybe
it's the stress, maybe it's my job, maybe it's always trying to please
everyone, maybe it's my age, maybe it's . . .

Jeez, stop whining.

Today is Saturday. Monday is my birthday. I'll be 43. I'm already
halfway through my life — if I'm lucky. I need rest. It's a big weekend for me. My wife and daughter are going on a two-day camping
trip with a YMCA group, which means I'll have the whole place to
myself. This is a good thing. I'll be able to channel surf, work on the

hot rod, go without shaving, pee in the bushes when I please, and have precious time to think.

Of course, since I'm wide awake, I guess *now's* as good a time as any to start thinking. When I think, it's usually about something big, like how to accessorize my lawn tractor, or how to get a few extra horsepower out of the garbage disposal.

At least that's what I used to think about. Now, because of this mid-life thing, my attention has been diverted to thinking about the big questions that everyone asks when they suddenly realize they're not going to live forever.

"Who am I?"

"Why am I?"

"Where do I go from here?"

"Just where *is* here?"

"Can I still hear?"

To try and answer these questions I've started reading a lot. Not fiction, exactly. Or philosophy. Different stuff. I have one of the books on my nightstand right now.

It's about quantum physics.

At first this stuff was really exciting. I absorbed everything I could get my hands on. My reading list was sort of *The Celestine Prophecy of Motorcycle Maintenance Embraced by the Light on the Road Less Traveled by the Dancing Wu Li Masters of Hyperspace*. I know. I'm on a roll. I can't seem to stop. I'm on a personal quest to resolve big issues. I want the answers to the big questions. And just for old times sake I want to know how to squeeze more garbage into smaller cubes in the trash compactor.

The book I'm reading now, *The Tao of Physics*, says that no matter what well-known laws of physics apply to us and our everyday world, that at a subatomic or quantum level the rules are, well . . . different. Normally, I couldn't care less, but now, as a man at mid-life, this really bothers me. Apparently, these teeny particles that, incidentally, no one can see, can be in two places at the same time.

I can't do that.

They can travel back and forth in time.

Can't manage that, either, although I've hurt myself trying.

Also, sometimes they're particles and sometimes waves and sometimes both at once, which means that they are at one location and *everywhere* at the same time.

Now *that* would be really neat to do because it would completely eliminate boredom and the exorbitant cost of today's air fares. I could catch every major sporting event, go to every great party, witness every great volcanic eruption, and be abducted nightly by aliens without ever leaving the house.

Weirdest of all, quantum physicists say that unless certain conditions are met, these subatomic particles don't *actually* exist. At least I *think* that's what they're saying. These are pretty complicated concepts, and suggest a very different view of things. In the books I'm reading they leave out a lot of the math and heavier proofs, the stuff I wouldn't understand without going to college for five more years.

Here's my big problem: Since, at the most basic level we're just a bunch of quantum particles, I hope this doesn't mean what I'm afraid it does, that in some very scary way, *I'm not really here.*

Now for the bad news: If I'm not really here, neither are you. It's a lot more complicated, but the bottom line is that if we're not really here, then nothing we think, say, or do means anything, right? What's the point of being good? Why do I spend two hours at the gym every day? What really happened to that delicious steak I ate for dinner?

This stuff is enough to keep anyone up at night, particularly a guy like me, who is too close to his mid-40s. That's the fulcrum. But I don't want to get into that at the moment.

It's 3:54 a.m. I've got to get some sleep.

Don't think I'm not trying. My eyes are closed, but my clock's face is so bright that the time five minutes ago is still burned into my retinas.

Clocks have always been a part of my life.

My Grandma's electric clock had a metal panel in back that said DO NOT TOUCH! If you sat in a chair with your feet off the ground, touched it, and then touched someone else, the electricity would fly. My brothers and I had lots of fun playing Shock-a-Sibling.

"Dave, come over here a minute. Grab my shoulder."

"Ow! God, what is that?"

We'd did this for hours, until we accidentally touched Grandma, affecting her pacemaker in such a way that she launched into twenty minutes of a really impressive rhumba.

When I was a little older, I got one of the first AM/FM clock/radios with a sleep timer. You remember those? It was great waking up to rock and roll. Then there was the purple clock radio with the two dials that looked the same. You thought you were changing the station. You were really setting the alarm for 2 a.m. Next, I got one of the first-generation digitals, with those Rolodex-style flipping platters that fell over every minute, like little Olympics judges lived inside. There's nothing like trying to sleep with the sound of crashing plastic in your ear. Then I got a glowing red digital, but I didn't keep it long. Because I'd seen every James Bond flick it just gave me anxiety dreams about disarming the damn thing before it blew up the world.

My current timepiece is a sterile humorless unit I bought to tide me over until the next wave. I've had it six years. Pathetic, right?

But it was heavily discounted.

I finally fall out hard at 5:27 a.m. and sleep soundly right up until the alarm buzzes at 5:30 a.m. Amazing how refreshed you can feel on three minutes' sleep. They say that during sleep the body repairs and regenerates itself. Three minutes is long enough for healing half a shaving nick and some minimum toenail growth. Nonetheless, it's time to get up. The girls need to meet the bus in the YMCA parking lot at 8:00 a.m., so it's time to start moving.

*

ROLLING OVER CAREFULLY, my feet hit the floor and I instinctively reach for my lower back. Lately, the word "chronic" has taken on real meaning. The whole ritual of waking bothers me. Also, going to bed. I even have trouble getting into and out of the shower. Maybe transitions just bother me. I think this aging thing is going to cause problems.

Next stop, the bathroom. Some mornings it sounds like I'm pouring a 12-quart pitcher nonstop into the bowl. I have to look in the mirror because I'm afraid that overnight I might have turned into some barnyard animal.

My wife's absolute favorite morning ritual of mine is throat-clearing. Women don't do this. They have noses and mucus, but my guess is they somehow amortize the phlegm buildup by quietly going "ah hem" all day long. My grunting and coughing wakes her up and I hear Laura call from the bedroom, "Timmmm!" as if I'm doing it on purpose. Then it's into and out of the shower. Quickly.

Laura is still in bed when I finish my routine. I love her, but I wish she'd get up and get going so I can have the place to myself.

For the entire weekend.

R-R-R . . .

*

NOW THAT I'M UP, there are chores to be done.

First, take the dog outside. This is a dog I said no to, but fell in love with anyway. We named her Spot due to the large black spot that covers her entire body. Black Labs are generally known for this particular marking. We keep her in a little kennel in the house. We'd let her run free but Spot has a problem. Much like her name, she leaves little spots. We tried all the housebreaking tricks, but nothing worked. We were so frustrated that we took her to the vet.

It's a good thing we did. He told us she was sick and that she needed a liver shunt — whatever that is. The vet also says that without a risky operation Spot might not live very long. If that isn't sad enough by itself, it's worse because Spot is my daughter's puppy.

Then why doesn't she feed it and take care of it? Just an observation . . .

I hope nothing bad happens to Spot. I had enough trouble trying to explain to Kady, she's six now, about the impermanence of living things and the theory of entropy when her fish, Carole, died two years ago.

Besides, you can't just flush a puppy. Well, you can. There are certain toilets I've used — the one in prison comes to mind — that would suck down a pony. Cons used to let it inhale full-sized towels just for fun.

At the back door, Spot and I do the big hug thing. But when I unlock the slider I realize I've forgotten to shut off my home security system. Spot yelps while I race across the house to disarm the ear-splitting screech. On the way I whack my little toe on the corner table. I always whack the same toe. By now you'd think it would be smart enough to get out of the way. I guess that's why the call it "the little toe." The pain forces me to do the one-legged "whee, whee, whee" hop all the way to the back door, where I hustle Spot out.

While Spot takes care of business I can see the sun peek over the horizon. The clouds are pink and this looks to be a very pretty day.

*

DID I MENTION that I have on no clothes?
I know. The first thing most people do when they get up — my wife, certainly; the Nordic 20-year-old twin girls next door, unfortunately — is put something on. Not me. It just seems more

natural to walk around on a brand new morning, in a half dark house, with nothing between me and Mother Nature but my good intentions. It would be great to answer the door this way when the studio limo and driver comes to take me to the set . . . but I don't have a limo or a driver, making this fantasy nearly impossible However, the UPS girl . . .

There's still time to watch the early news before I have to get my daughter up, so I turn on the little television in the kitchen. I may be naked, but I'm not worried about the newscasters seeing anything because Big Jim and the Twins (Ping and Pong) are hidden below the counter. Even I know where to draw the line. You'll never catch me watching TV this way in front of the big set in the den.

The news begins with the murder of the day. What a great way to kick off the morning, but let me ask you something: There's got to be more births than deaths, right? Wouldn't we be a lot better off if we began the day with pictures of happy parents with new babies?

Here in L.A. — and probably where you live, too — the weathermen were apparently born with names like Dallas Raines and Johnny Mountain. Pretty soon it will be Brian Blizzard, Claude Cloude and, best of all, Getitwrong N. Stillgitpade. I don't even know why we need weathermen in most places. Do we? What can they really say about weather in the southwest? Its degree of sun, the angle of the sun, when the sun is coming up, when the sun is going down, what the sun looks like, what to look for if you've missed the sun, how to recognize the sun if you've never seen it before.

"And in case you're from out of state, the sun is that bright, hot yellow thing in the sky. Don't look at it directly for too long, folks."

Go to the Northwest and it's all about rain.

In Alaska, you can pretty much say, "It's going to be cold and white and if you're a wuss . . . unpleasant."

Next up is the cheerful California Highway Patrol officer standing against a freeway system backdrop, telling us that every car in Los Angeles is moving along at a standstill. Why am I not surprised?

I have a great idea: Why not combine the weather map with the freeway map, and show the murders and tragedies with push pins? That way we can get it over all at once.

My biggest problem with the newscasts is that I don't understand why all of life is divided into news, weather, and death. This seems a little out of balance. I'd really like a segment on what I should have for breakfast.

"Good morning. Brice Krispies here with the breakfast report. This morning, as a bit of a challenge, try shredded wheat without milk. And tomorrow, simply a banana shake. On the weekend live it up with a dash of cinnamon in your Kona coffee, and if you feel really daring, try a cinnamon bun."

Brice is right about those cinnamon buns. They're not only good, but good for you. If you want to die soon. Each one contains 800 grams of fat, the same as a Big Mac and a hot dog. Or two pork chops and mashed potatoes with a healthy pat of butter. Many of us eat a hearty American breakfast of bacon, eggs, and hash browns and *then* polish it off with a cinnamon bun. There should be a warning on the package: "Do not eat if you have a heart condition or if you want to avoid one." Also, "If you have circulation problems, don't even *open* the cellophane." And, finally, "Okay, we warned you." No human can eat one of these a week and live. But if you do survive, this load of fat and calories can easily be burned off by drinking a gallon of grapefruit juice and climbing Mount Everest with the Anvil of the Gods strapped to your back. Sorry, walking up and down the stairs or to your car just won't do it.

Cinnamon buns are not only hard to resist, but hard to keep in their original shape. Get them home quickly because within twenty minutes they slowly disintegrate into their constituent fat molecules. You have to eat it fast or it loses its shape and melts into a clear, mucus-like substance. It's not really a pastry, but reconstituted beef fat and beef talon. It's just dusted with flour. Not that I'm complaining, because I love the things.

Do you know what else would be helpful? Ideas about what clothing to wear. I can never figure out my guy-type ensembles, but if I knew that two salesmen from Barneys would be on each morning to give me wardrobe tips, I'd be there.

Anything would be better than the wife saying, "You're going out in that?"

"No, I just want to see if I still fit in these shirts. This is just a trial."

I could also use some practical guy advice. "Instead of rushing around groggy in the morning trying to find the things you have to take to work tomorrow, put them in your car the night before." Or, "Remember, khakis go with everything."

I'm just killing time. I wish the girls would get up.

Maybe I should put on some pants.

*

I WOULD RATHER PICK UP dog mines in the backyard than wake up difficult people. I understand, because as a kid I would have sold my grandmother for a few more minutes in the sack snuggling with the great white biscuit. My wife is impossible. It is only safe to wake her from a distance, like Portugal.

I always try to rouse Kady with an exciting thought so that she just pops up ready to go. (Amazing how kids can do that without any coffee.) I usually kiss her, and say something like, "I dreamed about being trapped in the Venezuelan jungle."

She'll say, "Gee, Dad, this is getting creepy. That's the third time this week."

Actually, I don't say that, but I do try to get her brain active. "Hey, I dreamed about pigs flying."

She'll say, "I didn't dream at all."

Then I know I've got her. "Why not?"

"I didn't want to dream because I didn't want to come in and visit you two." Lately she's had strange dreams and ends up in our bed.

Now, I'm standing in her doorway without a shirt on, teasing, "Well, I'm going to work now."

"You can't."

"Why not? I'm late."

"You can't go to work like that because people can see your belly."

We both laugh and she's up.

*

I'M WONDERING HOW REAL or unreal the world of dreams is compared to our waking world. The Hindus and Buddhists say that our every day world is an illusion called Maya and what I've been reading about quantum physics seems to support that. I mean, right now, as I sit here in the kitchen waiting for Kady and Laura, my butt and the chair it's resting on both seem pretty solid, right? It's a solid butt/chair relationship. The physicists tell us that matter is almost totally *empty space*, so to them my butt (and the chair) look like the view of the heavens from the bridge of the Starship Enterprise. In addition, because on the micro-level there are supposedly no definite hard line borders between anything anyway, from that perspective my butt also kind of blends with the chair like cheese on a cheeseburger.

This is almost enough to put me off of eating fast food ever again. Sheesh . . . I don't like it when my kid has nightmares and now I'm going to have some.

*

LAURA RUSHES into the kitchen while I'm making breakfast for my daughter: cereal and milk with a dash of half-and-half. Anything to get the kid to eat. We have to leave to meet the bus in thirty minutes, and no one is really ready. Kady still needs to get dressed, which means she'll try on different outfits for fifteen minutes and complain about not being able to do a thing with her hair. Women! I also need to finish dressing and deal with my impossible hair.

Out of nowhere, my daughter announces that she doesn't want to go camping. That really bums me out. I've been looking forward to being alone for the weekend. Laura's also bummed because now that means a little argument. And as I expected, the girls begin snapping at each other. I'd step in and try to stop it but that would be wrong, because then they will find a way to blame me for everything. This goes on until Laura looks at me and says, "I've got such a headache."

"Motrin IB, Mom," Kady says. "The pain stops here."

Laura laughs and raises an eyebrow. "She's right. But she still watches way too much TV."

While they settle things I look through the laser disc cabinet to find a couple films for tonight's audience of one. *Forbidden Planet* looks good. Now all I need is a companion feature, but my view is suddenly blocked by a sheet of paper Laura has thrust in front of my face.

"What's that?" I ask.

"It's the list of stuff I need you to do while we're gone."

One part of me resents this because it takes away from the things that I thought I was going to do. The other part resents it also.

"Don't forget to call the plumber," she says. "He can come over this afternoon. And remember to pick up the clothes from the dry cleaner." She means *her* clothes; my fancy t-shirts are all machine washable. "And someone's going to drop by with tile samples for the new house. Just pick one."

"How do you decide between seven shades of sand?"

"Choose whatever you like."

"Mohave? Gobi? Sahara? Just remember you said that. What else?"

"Feed the dog."

"You have to *tell* me this?"

"I know how much you hate the smell."

"I'll live. I'll gasp for air, but I'll live."

"And you know about the medication?"

"Okay, tell it all to me again."

"She eats three times a day. Half of the can in the morning, quarter of the can in the afternoon with just kibble, but no water. And a quarter can at night. And make sure she gets outside."

"What about the medicine?"

"Make sure she takes her pills. Two pills at the first feeding, two pills at the second feeding and put that gel on at the evening feeding."

"Okay. I've got it. Two cans in the morning . . . "

"Can't you hear me? Half a can in the morning!"

"I was just having a little fun . . . "

I don't know why she worries. The dog will get fed, even if I don't do it exactly as she would have. Spot may get her gel in the morning and the pill sometime during the Nightly News, but I promise she'll at least be alive when the girls get home.

"Oh, and put the cat out at night."

"We have a cat? Wait, we do have a cat. I've seen her. Her name is . . . Player." (Our daughter named it because the cat plays. The cat couldn't really argue because she also does other things, and it could have been worse.)

"Congratulations, you *do* live here. By the way, I left a chicken breast and thigh in the fridge for you . . . "

"That's sweet. But you know I'm not attracted to chicken."

" . . . and a casserole. You just put the rice in that sauce, and add the peppers to it. Then you take off the chicken skin, cut the chicken into pieces . . . "

I'm lost.

" . . . put it in a frying pan, turn on the stove . . . "

Laura plans meals for me. It's her way of being nice, but it just ain't going to happen. I don't have the heart to tell her that I've *already* planned my favorite meal: a bologna sandwich. And none of that low-fat, plasti-wood, leather-look vinyl garbage, because one day while on the golf course I overheard a physicist tell someone that if you eat enough low-fat fake bologna and fake low-fat cheese food, and add a pop tart, that you can pass a transistor. It's all basically linoleum in the end. So I'm going to make it on Wonder Bread and put potato chips right on the sandwich. And I'll have a Classic Coke. The last time I fixed one of these beauties, Laura caught me red-handed. She said, "You're going to eat that?"

"No, this is a sample lunch. I'm just trying it out before I make my real lunch. But there's no sense wasting the good stuff."

When the girls are gone, I'm not even going to set the table. If Laura was here by herself, she would actually put out place settings with utensils in the correct spots, arrange fresh-cut flowers, eat a wonderful dinner, and do the dishes *that night*.

*

I'M READY TO GO but, as usual, I'm still waiting for the girls. So I'll look on the bright side: This gives me a couple minutes to slip into the garage to check out my "baby," a 1946 Ford I've been restoring. Anyone who lived then would have thought this car kind of ugly. It was no big deal, but I like it because it's got a big round back and fat fenders, plus I can take six people for a ride — whether they want to or not. I told my folks about the car, and I can't wait to take them for a spin when they come to visit. From up top the car may look original, but underneath it's running about 300 horses, disc brakes, and fully independent suspension. I always smile when I picture my folks smoking the tires and getting her sideways on an entrance ramp.

The car just *looks* like a memory, yet there's something about that memory I connect with: This car *had* a life, and has since been totally forgotten. Maybe I can't restore the original magic, but I can make it better than it was. I can combine what used to be with something new and make it live forever.

You'll also be able to see this hot rod coming. I painted it candy apple red because, well . . . it's an outrageously juvenile color. Not very subtle. Very Sixties. Totally guy-like. Take the most macho guys and trick out a car and suddenly lime green, metallic purple, and candy apple red are their favorite shades. We become hairdressers. And house cleaners. The bottom of the car has to look as good as the top.

"Check out that oil pan. Clean enough to eat off of."

This early in the morning, the garage is still and cool and lonely. Later, when I get back, I'll open the big door, let the outside world in, and put the finishing touches on my hot rod. There are just a couple things to do, plus put on the hood ornament.

I might as well get it down now, while I've got a minute. I left it on the shelf above the work bench . . . which is where I'm looking now, which is . . . why isn't the box here? Wait . . . here's the box. Nope, this is not the box. Maybe it's behind this box. Uh uh. Maybe another box? How about this one? It's not in here, either. All these boxes look alike.

Laura pulls open the door from the house and pokes her head into the garage.

"We're ready."

Gotta go. I'll have to deal with this later.

*

W E'RE FINALLY on the way to the YMCA.
I've driven to the "Y" probably 200 times and yet some-how whenever I'm in the car with Laura, the power struggle for navigating starts immediately.

"I think you should take the freeway," she says.

"No, I'm just going to go down Ventura."

It's a no-win situation. If there's any trouble on Ventura, she'll say "I told you to take the freeway." If I try the freeway, which I don't want to do, and it's jammed up, she'll say "You should have stuck with your instincts."

Like most decisions in life, this is one best not to over-think. You just decide, stick with it, and move on.

So I take the freeway — and it's jammed. Now I'm mad at myself, she and the kid are mad, and the car grows unusually quiet.

Fortunately, I have all weekend to take any road I like and do anything I want.

*

W E PULL INTO THE "Y" parking lot. Kady sees a girlfriend and runs over to talk. Laura stays in the car with me.

"I'm going to spend a whole weekend with 16 little girls and their moms," she moans. "What was I thinking?"

"You mean you'd rather stay with me?"

"No. I just wonder what I was thinking."

"Kady wanted to do this. You like to do things together. I'm jeal-ous. I wish I could go."

"Okay. You go."

"Ah . . . I'd love to but, you know, I've already made plans."

"Oh? What are you thinking?"

"Oh, nothing much. First I'll take care of all the items on your list. Very important. I'll probably work on the hot rod a bit. Then maybe I'll look for some Korean hookers, get a massage — a real massage — and invite the blonde 20-year-old twins next door over for a sunset hot tub."

"Well, have fun," Laura says, unfazed.

"Okay. So maybe I won't get the massage," I say.

"But you will play music really loud because I don't let you when I'm home. And watch movies until 3:00 in the morning, sleep all day, and eat horrible food."

She knows me so well. Maybe I can just leave the uneaten casserole in the refrigerator and she'll understand.

"Have fun. I love you," she says, and gives me a long, soulful kiss, clearly designed to make me forget the twin blondes next door. It seems to be working.

"And Tim . . . ?"

"Yes, dear."

"Do yourself a big favor and stop reading that book on your nightstand. And don't buy more. You're not getting any sleep, the pets are already spooked, and you're beginning to scare me. Read a novel. Or work in the garage instead. Put something together. And this time, read the manual first."

"But I have to figure out this stuff."

"No, you don't. It's got nothing to do with real life."

"But what if I'm not really here?"

"Feel that?" Laura says, punching my shoulder, hard.

"Ow!"

"You're here. But I'm leaving now. Have a nice weekend."

"I love you, too," I say. "Oh, did you pack the cell phone?"

"Yes."

"Did you bring a good flashlight?"

"Yes."

With that, we get out, unload the bags and join the other kids and their parents. I'm not sure I'd want to be the driver on that bus.

I can see it now: Twenty women going, "Left. Left! No, you take the freeway!"

Even more worrisome, I'd be distracted, specifically by Shirley Johnson's butt. Nice. I used to see her at the gym all the time — along with some of the other moms and dads — but what can you tell through baggy sweat pants? She looks great in makeup. Maybe I *would* want to be the driver.

I give the girls a big hug and kiss and watch them climb aboard. I also peek around Laura to catch another glimpse of Shirley.

*

As soon as the bus pulls out of the lot, the urge to do a triple low fist pump overcomes me. "All right! I'm free. This is going to be great. It's just me!" While I am dancing and flailing, the other dads look at me from a distance like I'm either some kind of freak, or being hassled by a bee. I don't care what they think. I'm enjoying my little dance of joy on the blacktop.

I'm in the mood for breakfast. A real breakfast. Double helpings of sausage, eggs, and toast. Maybe a cinnamon bun. Forget the yogurt Laura left me. And that cereal no one can pronounce. Mooselips. Mouse Licks. No matter how good it is, if I can't pronounce it I'm not about to eat it. And this afternoon I'll go to the speed shop and hang out with the guys. And maybe I will get that massage.

Yes, I'm in a pretty good mood.

Until I get to my car. The way the light hits the driver's door it looks like there's some kind of ding. There is: A big ding and some little dings around it, like planets around a sun. Now how did that get there? I've only been parked for twenty minutes. This really irritates me. Who would do something like that and not leave a note with a full explanation?

To tell the truth, me! One night long ago I was out drinking and howling with my buddies. Somehow I got it into my head to run across a row of car hoods. Don't ask me why. Then I slipped and slammed down on one hood so hard that the air cleaner impression came straight up through the sheet metal. I almost broke my back. When I recovered, my pals said, "Go in there and find the owner and tell him."

"I'm not going to do that," I said. "He's got insurance."

On the way home everybody in the car was mad at me. "You ass. Why didn't you do the right thing?"

Didn't want to take the responsibility, is why. Decided to act like I'd never really been there. Now I realize that what goes around comes around. Karma's found me and paid me back. I've only got a ding. I should consider myself lucky.

Maybe I should try to find the guy whose car I ruined. The restaurant probably has its old reservation book. It was only twelve years ago. Nah. But at least my heart's in the right place.

This bit of remorse doesn't do much for my mood, though. Suddenly, the music on the radio doesn't sound so great, the day doesn't look so wonderful.

I think I'll just go home and work on the hot rod.

*

THIS TIME, just because I want to, I take Ventura Boulevard home, instead of the freeway. It's jammed.

That's okay. The slow pace gives me the chance to consider and rank the many activities available to a single married man on the loose for the weekend.

I believe we all have different aspects of our personalities inside our heads, vying for attention, though some are more troublesome than others. The young boy in me wants to get right to the fun stuff. Shop for TVs, test drive cars, go to a matinee, eat junk food. This will only kill a couple hours. The adult wants to take care of the many chores Laura left for me. But it's really not what's on my mind. I need to look under the heading, "What Men Do When Their Wives Are Out of Town," cross-referenced with "What Men Think They Can Get Away With."

Immediately, the words "other women" pop into mind. That's my bad self speaking. Sometimes I like him.

Another thing about getting older: Even if I had the inclination, who has the energy? Besides, one sobering thought sticks with me: All the women I know and really like are on the bus with my wife and daughter.

Of course, there are always strip clubs, but who the hell is stripping at 8:30 in the morning? I don't think I want to know. Even if I drive 30 miles to the nearest strip bar and see a sign that reads, "Live Nude Girls," I'd have to be honest with myself: At this time of morning it's just going to be the bartender, the bouncer, and me — and I'm not taking anything off! Anyway, strip clubs are all about frustration. It's kinda like going to a buffet restaurant where you can look at the food but . . . HEY! DON'T TOUCH THAT!

These days I just *look* at the young women. I can't help myself. And according to *science* I'm not supposed to help myself — even though the "biology-is-destiny" excuse never works with Laura. Let me paraphrase something I once read in *Newsweek*: Did you know that before puberty and after menopause women have essentially the same waistlines? But between those times, while guys are supposed to be filling out like prehistoric hunters, a woman gains nearly 35 pounds of so-called reproductive fat around her hips and thighs? And I'm *supposed* to look at those curves because it's our species' way of signaling reproductive potential. According to a University of Texas psychologist, "You have to get very close to see the details of a woman's face, but you can see the shape of her body from 500 feet — and it says much more about mate value."

I'll say!

Sometimes Laura catches me looking. I just tell her it's no big deal. "Think of it as me visiting the Museum of Natural Beauty and they're the fine artwork." She lets me get away with this because I think she knows that my real problem is that I'm too old and too married for any of this. I'd have to be about twenty-five to have something to talk about with these women. But twenty-five seems so far away. Had I married and had kids early, like my brother, these women could be my daughters. Or his daughters. Oh, oh.

I'm hungry. I never stopped for that breakfast. Now, a hamburger sounds good. Do they serve hamburgers this early? Soon it will be too late for breakfast, but it's still too early for lunch. This seems to me to be the main feature lately of my whole life: too old to do this, too young to do that. Too awake to do this, too tired to do that. Too busy to do this, too . . . well, I'm always busy. Honestly, I don't even really feel like eating right now. Eating is no fun when you've got to watch your cholesterol. Trying to remember to eat right just gives me an anxiety attack.

What would my wife do if she was on her own for the weekend? She'd go shopping. Maybe I should go and buy a Ferrari. Or I could check out the gadget store. I'd pretty much buy anything that comes in Styrofoam packing, or that says, "digital," "all steel construction," or "240K" on the box.

Maybe I should go to the gym and work out. Nah. I could just cruise around, but idle time is the devil's time. Suddenly the truth hits me hard in the gut: I have absolutely nothing to do. My big plans have evaporated, along with my energy.

That means it's back to the house for a bowl of Mouse Micks and skim milk. Then maybe I'll tinker with the hot rod.

I check the gas gauge. Half full. I floor it and take off, wishing more things were happening.

*

A S I PULL UP to an intersection, I see a homeless man muttering to himself on the corner. He seems young; too young to be homeless. Maybe he's just dressed that way for fun. He's bundled up for winter, even though autumn has just begun and Indian summer is still in the air. His space is littered with his belongings. Wait. I think I recognize him. Didn't he once run comedy programming at the network?

It must be strange to suddenly not have a roof over your head. The thought of how quickly things can change or go wrong in life is scary. There are so many things I would like to ask this guy about his experiences. I would also really like to know where he got that great American Indian blanket.

Oh, great. He must have seen me staring at him because he's heading this way. Okay. So I'll pull a couple bucks from my wallet, roll down the window, and hand them over.

"Here you go, buddy."

He snatches them, looks at the bills, looks back at me, and says, "Did you buy the eggs?"

"What?"

"Eggs. Did you buy the eggs?!"

"I'm sorry, I, uh, don't know . . . "

"You *do* know. You know the answers. You. You have them all."

"Look, I gave you three dollars," I say, quickly rolling up the window. "Get a whole carton."

With that he flips out, curses, and starts stomping on the sidewalk. Only a thin sheet of glass separates us. My heart races at the thought of what he might do next.

The light turns green. I floor it, looking back to watch this nutcake still fuming. Then I turn around to see where I'm going and . . . holy shit!

I slam on the brakes as fast as I can. The anti-lock hits, the back end slides out. I tap the curb and almost jump it, just missing a trash can.

I am very lucky. A split second slower reaction time and I'd have plowed into a mom walking two children across Ventura Boulevard. Can you imagine doing anything more horrible? And it's all because I'm not paying attention to the world around me.

I try to apologize but the young mother is too shook up and

mad to listen. She can only glare at me and try to stop her kids from crying. A pedestrian who offered to help turns to me and says, "Didn't you see her?"

"It was my fault. I should have been looking at what I was doing." I feel like I'm going to throw up.

Fortunately everyone's okay. The damage to my car is incidental, not that it would matter to me if it had been totaled. Anything is better than the alternative. The mom and her kids cross the street and disappear into a drug store. The crowd disperses. One guy wants an autograph and a picture with me.

From the corner of my eye I see the homeless guy across the street. He points an accusing finger at me. But when I spin around, he's not there.

I slide into the driver's seat, start the engine, and drive slowly toward home. I don't know why, but for some reason I check the gas gauge again.

Now it reads half empty.

TWO

TWENTY MINUTES later I coast into the driveway and turn off the engine.

I'm still in shock. Who wouldn't be? This is what I get for talking to some weird guy with a great blanket instead of paying attention to the road. I'm really unbelievably lucky.

I should probably just go inside, but I can't seem to move. I'm stuck in place, unable to stop thinking about how life, in one instant, can drastically change direction. The more I struggle, the more I stay in place. My heart beats wildly, I panic, and suddenly I realize the awful truth: I haven't unbuckled my seat belt!

Maybe I should just take that as a sign and stay in the car. Besides, I can't stop thinking about my almost-accident. Why didn't it happen? Was my reaction time just quick enough? Did a greater force stop it, or did I just get lucky? Maybe it has nothing to do with me. Maybe they just got lucky. And just what is luck? Perhaps if I sit here long enough, watching my neighbor mow his lawn, I'll come up with the answer. I might also figure out why he does it himself when his very expensive Japanese gardener comes every Wednesday. On the other hand, this might just be my way of doing anything to keep from having to feed the dog.

*

WHEN STUFF LIKE THIS happens I slip into a mental question and answer period that reminds me of my college philosophy class. The professor never had any definite answers, but he wouldn't accept that as an excuse not to ask the questions. So here's my question: Do we have free will, or are our lives predetermined?

I can already feel my head spinning like a lonely proton in a super-collider. But I have to know: Can we actually choose what we do, or has God/The Void/tarot cards/Kenny Kingston already planned our existence down to the most minute detail? Am I asking this question because I want to, or because it was already predetermined that I'd sit in my driveway and make myself insane?

Let's see: It's natural to want to feel I have free will and that I can make my own decisions. That's how the ego protects us. Otherwise, why would I even get out of bed and go to work in the morning? At the very least, I control *some* of my actions, like which excuse I'll use when I show up late for the job, not that this ever happens.

Recently, I surfed the World Wide Web, to check out what people thought about this topic. I ran across a note from a woman named Eve. She said she believed free will existed because we control our own thoughts. According to her theory, if she could think of something that wasn't being influenced directly by her senses — say, radishes, when no radishes were around — then it proved she had free will. So that must mean that wherever I am, whenever I want, I am free to imagine whatever I choose: a great dinner, a hot date, no remorse in the morning. And I can do this even if the food is lousy, the romance nonexistent, and I'm pissed at myself for shelling out $200 for nothing.

Remember, the key word is "imagine."

The other side of this classic argument is that everything is predetermined and I never make any independent choices in life. Whatever happens is supposed to happen and if I don't like it that's tough. This also seems to make sense: After something happens, it's the *only* thing that happened, right? *Could have, would have,* and *should have,* they mean absolutely nothing. In retrospect it's easy to say that's the way it *was meant* to be.

Damn . . . what if my "choices" *are* nothing more than what I'm destined to do, always have done, and always will do? What if I'm the robot slave of an extraterrestrial intelligence who created our world in some sort of cosmic petri dish and now sits back in his alien Barcalounger, watching my life, as written, like some bad sitcom? That's my Alien Puppet Master theory. It's a little over the top but I'm refining it.

I can't say for sure, but I don't think free will is just an illusion. Think of it like a stand-up comedian would: God sets up the situation or joke, but lets you choose the punch line. Then it's just like being on stage: Either you get a laugh or you don't, but you have to move on and choose again. Unfortunately that seems like determinism. Also sounds a lot like my stand-up career.

Maybe it's a good thing that we can't figure out this stuff because then we'd be able to know the future, which would definitely take the fun out of life, except for about five minutes at the high-stakes blackjack tables.

*

T HE SERIOUS DOWNSIDE of this pondering is that I'm always reminded about the car accident that killed my dad. I was eleven. That was my first experience with how *my* life could change abruptly, and transform me completely in the process.

When my dad died, I kept blaming myself. I slowed the whole event and looked at all the details. I imagined how things could have been in a million different ways. But I couldn't change a thing, so in the end I felt powerless and stupid. I think I was not guilty as much as pissed.

If only I'd talked to him some more that morning instead of rushing off to my friend's house.

If only I'd hidden the car keys.

If I'd delayed him for just a minute or an hour. Would the drunk driver who killed my dad have killed someone else — or no one at all?

Of course all of this is based on the naive assumption that I could have somehow stepped out of life for a moment, seen what was happening, come back, told everybody, and made things happen the way I wanted. If I could have, maybe then I wouldn't feel so frustrated. If I could have, I would now be wearing a sequined suit, with a sell-out show in Vegas. It's sad knowing that after something happens, every option to change the past is gone. There's no such thing as a second chance at the same thing, except in *It's A Wonderful Life* and certain episodes of the *Twilight Zone*. Many times, growing up, there were questions I'd have liked to ask my father. Now I'm older than my dad was when he died. I wonder where I'd be in life if he'd stayed around.

I have often wished to be able to visit the alternate dimension or universe where events played out a little differently or where all the other choices we could have made exist.

The first thing I'd do is find my dad. The second is, I'd find out what would have happened if I'd ditched my high school film lab and gone to Denise's house when she asked me to come over. I knew what she had in mind, but I was busy editing a student film and kept putting her off. I promised to come over as soon as I finished. Eventually she called and told me to forget it. I chose the film over her. I was an idiot.

I might even meet myself in the parallel universe, since we both like to hang out at the same places. If I know myself, and I do, I'll give myself a hearty pat on the back, and whisper in my ear: "Tim, there's only room for one of us in this universe.

"G'night everybody."

Even if I could be in two places at once, I obviously shouldn't be.

*

OKAY, SO PEOPLE may not bump into themselves in alternate universes, but in quantum physics lots of strange stuff still happens. For instance, there's the Schrodinger's Cat paradox. Trying to think your way through this well-known thought experiment, devised in 1935 by Nobel Prizewinning physicist Erwin Schrodinger, really illustrates the manic and magical nature of cutting edge physics — and why I can't get any sleep at night.

Schrodinger asked us to imagine a cat sealed in a box. With the cat is a capsule of poison, a radioactive substance like uranium, a Geiger counter, and a hammer. The experiment lasts an hour. If, within that time, an atom of the uranium decays, the Geiger counter triggers the hammer, it smashes the capsule, and the poison kills the cat. If it doesn't decay, nothing happens.

Doesn't sound too complicated. Wait an hour, open the box, and see what happened to the cat. Meanwhile, sometime during the test the cat has either died or not, right?

Not exactly.

The experiment is set up so that the uranium atom has a 50-50 chance of decaying. According to the rules of quantum physics — which, because of the unpredictable nature of subatomic particles, deals only with *probabilities* in the so-called micro-world, instead of the simple action-reaction model of our macro-world — the radioactive atom has something called a "wave function" that consists equally of a decayed state and an undecayed state. Therefore, until the box is opened, the odds of an event within the box are even, and it is statistically impossible to predict which of the states is the atom's final one, not to mention the cat's health.

This can also be thought of in another, somewhat perverse way: If, as Schrodinger insists, we know nothing about the cat until we open the box, then until we do the cat is both dead and alive *at the same time*.

Unbelievable, right?

Either that or Schrodinger convinced the cat to sit very, very still.

To really understand Schrodinger's Cat one needs to grasp a few basic facts about physics, like the Heisenberg Uncertainty Principle. However, because I'm still sitting in my car, in the driveway, I have to explain without the usual books, charts, slide shows, guest lecturers, and laser pointers. So it could take a little time. Ninety seconds, tops.

The Uncertainty Principle explains why we can't determine the state of the uranium atom in on which Schrodinger's cat's life depends. It says that the reason things are uncertain in the quantum world, and probably everywhere else if you think about it, is because the observer alters the observed by the mere act of observation. That's why, in the quantum world, we really can't be sure of anything, like a particle's velocity, location, or opinion on gun control. Everything is based on the probability of occurrence. One reason probability rules is because subatomic particles are so small. In fact, the particles may not be particles at all, but waves that, for the moment, express themselves as particles just when we happen to be looking for them, otherwise, we wouldn't know where they are. This is much like when I'm supposed to be fixing things around the house, but I'm really lying on the couch watching TV. When I hear my wife's keys in the door, I'll quickly express myself as a handy man to help "the observer" identify me as such. Quanta are helpful that way.

Our way is to predict the existence of subatomic particles mathematically and *then* find them, but we can't find them unless we arrange for them to collide with other subatomic particles — which is why we spend so much money on super-colliders for the physicists to play with. And someone must be around to observe the collision and see the particles, or else we're just shit out of luck. Even if all three conditions are met — the particles, the collision, the observer — since one can only determine one of a particle's aspects (speed, location) at a time, and then only approximately, the other aspects are always uncertain. In other words, trying to measure one value of a quantum particle changes the other values, in addition to changing the value of the observed particle itself, which is why making predictions about these values is the best we can do — and this sounds so confusing.

Uncertainty also closely describes how many women act on a first date. Just when you're sure one thing is going to happen, something entirely different does. By trying to measure the speed and location of her particles you cause the observed to utter, "I don't think so, Tim." In layman's terms, it never pays to be a presumptuous bastard right off the bat.

Of course, one can measure many things about particle *board*, but that's not something I allow in my house.

Fortunately, the Uncertainty Principle is not limited only to quantum theory. It is clearly applicable in our day-to-day lives, in situations ranging from negotiating a book/movie/TV deal to unclogging your toilet.

Heisenberg won the Nobel Prize for Physics in 1932, for his Uncertainty Principle. His former home is now a museum, but it doesn't get many visitors. Possibly that's because the brochures can only say that Heisenberg "may have" slept there.

What bothers me most — and this has a lot to do with my insomnia — is the idea that my subatomic constituents don't seem to play by the same rules I have to. That's a bit freaky and it doesn't seem fair, unless you're in politics, where it seems you can get away with anything while your constituents can go to hell. For instance, why can't I be in two places at once? I'd like to film an episode of *Home Improvement* every Friday night *and* be at home in bed with my wife at the same time. But that will never happen unless I'm a very lucky *muon* — one of many subatomic particles with a funny name, which explains why physicists often laugh for no apparent reason.

Of course, what worries *me* is whether or not I'm really here. In *The Tao of Physics*, author Fritjof Capra says subatomic particles don't really exist as bits of matter at a particular point in space, but rather that they are energy with a *tendency* to exist as matter — under certain conditions — in some places more than others. If I'm here, I suppose I satisfy those conditions, but if what I've read about uncertainty is true, that could easily change, right? I just can't be certain. Just because my wife slugs me and it hurts doesn't mean a thing. She might not be here either.

Someone please tell me to let it go. If I want frustration I can always turn on reruns of the OJ trial.

Or keep pondering the fate of Schrodinger's cat.

What most people don't realize is that crafty Schrodinger knew it was ridiculous to believe that the cat is both dead and alive at the same time. The probabilities involved only describe the quantum world, not the everyday world in which the cat lives (or dies). In fact, one problem with even talking about this stuff is that the language that we, the observers, use to describe our world is woefully inadequate in painting a clear picture of what we "observe" in the subatomic realm.

This paradox partly explains why Schrodinger just made up the Cat problem to screw with his physicist colleagues who liked to sit around drinking Schnapps and insist that the world only exists because we *think* it into existence. They must have believed it though, because after talking science for hours they'd try to "think" a detachment of young Austrian hookers into the room for a night of hide-the-quantum-bratwurst.

"Now you see it, now you don't, mein Fraulein."

Schrodinger may have had mischievous intentions, but the Cat paradox remains as popular and confusing as ever, even though some physicists now say they can easily disprove it because a mechanical measuring device will tell you right away if the cat's alive or dead. This comes in handy when you're trying to decide whether or not to go shopping for pet food.

Reading about the history of physics also has other pleasant dividends. For instance, I've discovered a rarely told part of Schrodinger's story: the truth about what happened after he published his thought-experiment. Apparently it worked too well and really angered and confused his peers. (Other sources report that they were pissed because they were so drunk on Schnapps the hooker experiment always failed.) These scientists decided to make Schrodinger's life miserable by, among other practical jokes, leaving dead animals on his front porch. According to the physicist's autobiography, the stress was so great that Schrodinger's doctor ordered him to take a sabbatical and forbade him to think about work. Schrodinger packed and left immediately for his lake-front cottage. When he returned, he realized he had forgotten all about the cat in the box. He rushed to open it and discovered that the cat had died. Schrodinger then made a brilliant deduction: Vacations cause cat death.

Unfortunately, he had borrowed his neighbor's cat for the experiment, and his garbled explanation of why proved even more convoluted than the Cat paradox. Schrodinger was laughed out of physics. Sadly, he spent his remaining years breeding sea monkeys in vacuum-sealed containers.

I can see my neighbor staring at me. He probably wonders why I've just been sitting in the car for the past 45 minutes.

"Is Tim dead? Alive? Do I have to rip open his car door to find out? Will doing that affect the outcome?"

As he walks over, I get out of the car quickly because I realize that any guy who rakes his leaves when he already has a gardener may be armed and dangerous. Anyway, it's time to go inside. I've got stuff to do.

Laura wants people to enter the house through the front door. But she's gone, so I get to do it the right way: through the garage. But first I'll fake like I'm going in the front, then do a couple stutter-steps to fool that ol' determinism, and head the other way.

*

THE PETS ARE WAITING in the kitchen when I walk inside. They want food again. They live the life of Riley. Well, of Riley's pets. Who *was* Riley, anyway? They can wait. It's only 9:30 a.m. and pets don't eat brunch. Okay, maybe poodles do.

Tell you the truth, I'm exhausted and a little distracted. There's a half-empty bottle of water on the counter. And a half-empty can of Lipton's sweetened tea that Kady only takes two sips of and leaves. Not too long ago I would have thought of both as half full.

I suppose this is a pretty recognizable perspective among the 40ish-plus men I know. It's like a common sigh. I talk with guys my age, and afterwards we all stop and take a deep breath together. And then we argue over who sighed the deepest or who sighed the longest. I mean, we're still men after all.

And we all know the truth: We can't make the journey again. It's like in those old movies where the pilot says, "I'm on this last mission and I've used so much fuel that I can't get back." Although sometimes I wish I could, I can't turn around and do my career — or life — over again. Maybe I can restore an old car's magic, but lately I feel that I don't have enough energy to re-create my own magic. Besides, I'm not sure that any new magic will seem magical enough. So for all intents this is it — and I'm left to consider the *quality* of life, and appreciate the spiritual things. Whoa boy, hold on to the reins.

It could be worse. A buddy recently told me, "Just wait until you're 54. What you go through then is even more scary because suddenly the tank looks only a quarter full!"

Everyone's a comedian these days.

I already feel my age. A few weeks ago I finally finished doing my last will and testament. There's a fun process. You talk about death with your wife and your lawyer, for a year, and about what everyone should do after you're gone, not to mention *do with you*. Everything's got to be perfect before you go. The last thing you want is to be in heaven, playing badminton with a cherub, and still be thinking, "Maybe I should have set up that trust fund differently."

I don't like this mood. But the truth is that I've been feeling this way off and on for some time. It's hard to say exactly what *it* is. I'm not depressed. I'm not unhappy. I'm not morose, melancholy, gloomy. Or even sad. It's an odd feeling. Lethargic? Listless? Phlegmatic? Cynical? Weary? Glum? Lifeless? Inanimate? Inert? Inorganic?

Dead?

Could be anything. What's the word I'm looking for? Confused? Insane? Narcissistic? Tedious? Humorless?

Malaise.

A funny word, but it seems to fit when I try it on — and it can easily be taken in if I lose a few pounds. Honestly, I'm not sure exactly what it means. I suppose I could look it up.

*

MY OFFICE IS AT the far end of the house. Actually, I share it with Laura. There are two computer desks made from the rare Ikea plant, which means old cardboard cartons pressed together really hard by two large Scandinavians.

My dictionary is so big that it has a stand and comes with its own tractor-trailer. I need a permit to move it from room to room. I've always loved dictionaries. I remember when I discovered my grandmother's unabridged volume. I must have been ten years old. The first thing I did was look up every swear word I knew. Oh, come on: You did it, too. "Shit" — in there. "Fuck" — oh, yeah. "Ass" — hey, more than one definition! That meant I could say it in polite conversation without getting grounded. The bigger the dictionary, the more the chance I'd discover something unbelievable. Had I used them, the number of forbidden words I found could have kept me in the principal's office indefinitely. I knew better, but it was still weird to see words *printed* that I wasn't allowed to say. I mean, why were they there in the first place? If they were so bad, shouldn't there at least have been some kind of Librarian General's warning that said that using them would tick off adults?

The way we treat words is odd. Words are combinations of letters. There's no inherent meaning. At best, they're our way of trying to describe reality and even then they are only an indefinite approximation. Words are maps to the territory of existence, and we shouldn't confuse the map with the territory.

Unfortunately, we often do.

My personal bitch is about the word "nigger." I don't like the word and I don't use it, but does that mean we have to call it the "N-word"? Are we really fooling anyone? Doesn't this just make the problem worse? It seems to me that by substituting one word for another we're actually giving the word more power than it deserves. We have power over words, not the other way around. If we're not careful then pretty soon we'll have to invent a whole bunch of new symbols to replace the old symbols; the trouble is, eventually they won't be any less objectionable.

Let's try something. "Hey, you freaking N-word!" Nope. Still hurtful. Doesn't change a thing for me.

Referring to people by their skin color in the first place conjures up too many difficult emotions. White equals light. Black equals dark. Good and evil. Sounds like immediate trouble. Ask yourself why, when you hear the news, it matters that four *black* men did something? They're not giving descriptions of the criminals so you can be on the lookout, they're just telling you their color, as if that had some meaning. I think that by using color terminology we *create* racial bias. We're used to "up and down," "good and evil," "black and white." But people with darker skin tones are *not* my opposite. In fact, I challenge anyone to tell me my skin color. Peach? Light tan? Crayola used to have a color called Flesh. They discontinued it because it was frankly racist, and, incidentally, never matched anyone's flesh color on this planet.

I tried an experiment around my house. We decided to try to call people by their color: milk chocolate, chocolate, peach, cinnamon. Believe me, it gets silly and pretty soon you want to call people by their names because you're sick of trying to figure out what color they are.

Of course, for me old habits die hard. So before I look up "malaise," I have to put on my reading glasses (a sure sign of midlife), and see if "anus," "breast," "boob," "booger," "butt," and "fart" are still in here. Some things never change. Some things are always fun.

*

Malaise, or mal ease\ *n*, [a French word, from the Old French, from *mal + aise* comfort — more at EASE] 1: an indefinite feeling of debility or a lack of health often indicative of or accompanying the onset of an illness. 2: a vague sense of mental or moral ill-being.

BINGO! NO WONDER THAT for no apparent reason I sit, on the edge of the bed in the mornings, for longer than I've ever sat.

Let's see what else is on this page. *Malachite*, the mineral. I've got a little statue made of malachite, and there's some in the hot rod hood ornament. *Malaysia*? It's where they invented malaise, of course. They breed it there, I think. I always thought I was German-Scottish, but now I think Malaysia is my ancestral home. They are my people. They are a tired people. They take great pride in their malaise, when they have the energy to give a damn. Maybe I should check with the Malaysian Embassy and see if I can talk with someone because, after all, they deal with this daily and might have some answers for me.

Oh, and here's *malarkey*, meaning insincere or foolish talk. Now who would do something like that?

*

IT'S ONE THING TO READ about malaise, another to feel it in your gut. I can't pinpoint exactly when it began, but I'm sure it was soon after the excitement over having the number one TV show, the number one movie, and the number one book — all at once — settled down. I'm not sorry it happened, but it did take up even more of the little time I have for my family. So I promised Laura I wouldn't do another movie during the next *Home Improvement* summer hiatus, in order to hang out with her and Kady.

So there I was, another season about to wrap, with no idea what to do next. It felt strange, but I plunged ahead.

In retrospect, I realize that for the first time since I did the *Tonight Show* in 1990, I took my foot off the career gas. I'd always kept it floored, but I eased back, and decided I had to get to the bottom of these feelings of . . . malaise *and* detachment. I figured one good way would be to start reading more on a subject that had always intrigued me: the nature of reality and the mysteries of existence. I wanted to know my place in the universe. So I returned to my passion for books about science and metaphysics.

Now, as we all realize, I'm in deep, deep trouble.

There is simply too much to consider. There are too many theories of creation, too many possible universes, too many phenomena that language can't explain. For all their power in day-to-day life, words *are* almost meaningless when trying to describe quantum events. We can only indicate meaning tangentially and through metaphor. I love my reading, but every time I think I've stumbled onto an Answer — a unified existential theory — another world to explore appears. I'd like to see the Energizer Bunny keep up this quest on just two AA batteries. Clearly, a side effect of the malaise is pure exhaustion. Add the worry that I might not really be here, and no wonder I'm wondering, "What's the point?"

After I'd read a couple of disturbing books, Laura noticed my moodiness and tried to cheer me.

"I know just how you feel. This happens to women all the time," she said. Then she gave me some practical advice: "Read something else!"

*

T HE OFFICE PHONE RINGS, dragging me back to — should I even say it? — reality.

"Hello."

"Mr. Allen?"

"Who's calling?" His voice sounds familiar, but you never know who gets your number. This guy could be trying to sell me something — like a case of worthless Woody the Cowboy dolls.

"Tom Carpenter from Celebrity Wheels."

"Oh, yeah. Hi Tom. What's up?"

"We're still trying to schedule picking up your car for this year's Celebrity Wheels car show. So I was wondering, could we come by Monday to get your rod?"

"Well . . . "

"We've kinda been waiting for you but, if not, we can do it another time."

"Oh, it's ready. Sure. I just gotta screw on the hood ornament. Sure. Come by."

"About nine a.m. Monday? Unless that's too early?"

"Too early? With a six-year-old?"

"OK. OK. See you then."

"Bye."

Great. Now I've got to finish that thing.

T HIS DETACHMENT AND MALAISE thing isn't just me. I had dinner in New York with my friend David and some other guys. We were all about the same age and successful. And feeling a bit lost.

Afterward, David and I went out on the balcony. It was a crisp New York City night. There we were, two grown men who had known each other for 25 years. He stared off into space. I stared in the opposite direction. I'm sure we wore the same expressions. I finally turned to David and said, "What is *your* problem?"

At first he said nothing — unlike him — and then he said, "I feel like . . . my paint box is running out of colors."

David's an artist, so he talks funny. I would have used a metaphor anyone could understand, like, "My gas tank's half empty." Still, he said what I'd been thinking.

"I'm not depressed — exactly," he continued. "It's just a sick feeling."

I told him about the malaise and the detachment and my personal research project. But as I spoke I could feel him become more and more confused. "I'm reading books about the loss of reality," I explained. "And now I'm afraid that nothing in life makes the least bit of difference. And even if it did, one day the sun is going to go nova and vaporize the Earth and what will any of this matter, anyway?"

"Jeez," said David. "Maybe we should just abandon our families, wear togas, and drink and party like Caligula."

"Because you are a good-looking gay man, that might be fine for you," I said. "But I'd have a problem with that because I don't want to be bathed by other men."

At that moment, our waiter walked onto the balcony. "You want to know what makes a difference?" he asked, with a knowing smile. We waited. "Not running out on your check." We should have expected that from him. He was young and had his whole life to look forward to. We had no choice but to toss him over the railing. He fell forty stories to his death. Lucky guy. No malaise for him.

"But why would you feel like this?" said David. "Look at how successful you are. You have a great job, a healthy family, you love your charities. What more could you ask for?"

David's reaction was understandable. Given the life I've had, people always think I should have a smile on my face and not a worry in my head. But what most people don't realize about success is that, as Garry Shandling once pointed out, you now have enough money to give yourself more time to worry about why you're miserable. That's not me, of course. I tried to make myself more clear to David. "It's like I'm in a race car and maybe I'm taking a curve too tightly, or following too close, so I let off the accelerator for a second. I'm not on the brakes or the gas, but right in the middle. It's a moment of weightlessness. I feel queasy. I'm still moving forward, carried by my momentum, but for a few seconds I know that I'm not totally in control. My concentration is broken and I can look around. But do I want to? Do I have any choice?"

"Good question," said David.

"Life is like the race," I continued. "The momentum carries us forward from childhood. But one day we wake up in the middle of our lives and we're shocked to find we're pushing or past 40. It's a weird zone. We take our feet off the gas to check it out. We notice the grandstand, the track, the pit, in a way we hadn't before, because we were focused on career and ambition, and providing for our families and staying alive. Next thing we know we're asking ourselves if we really want to race at all, what the race means, are there other races, who's really doing the driving, and what it means to win."

"Wow," said David. "If you weren't one of my oldest friends, I'd toss you off this balcony, too. You're making me feel worse."

Then we went back inside. It was obvious our friends had had a similar conversation. How else to explain the malaise in their eyes, the unfocused cognitive dissonance, the greenish pallor of unresolved nausea? Of course, since we'd all stuffed ourselves on raw oysters, flat meats in odd sauces, creme brulees, double-cognacs, and smoked big stinky cigars, it could point either way.

One of the guys suggested we cast off our moods and go dancing. Seemed like a good idea, so we changed into Spandex pants, sequined tops and heels, and painted the town candy apple red until the salmon-peach dawn broke over the metallic-black East River.

*

F OR THE FOLKS who may not be living through a mid-life crisis just yet, don't worry. You don't have to be left out. There are other signs of impending decrepitude of which you should be aware, until you either die early or the malaise creeps up and gets you, too.

For instance, there's ear hair. Now what is that all about? Isn't the hair growing on our head, faces, chests, arms, legs, back, butt, and genitals enough? It has to grow where we hear, too? And so strategically placed that we're the last ones to know?

I found out about ear hair a couple years ago when I went to the Sharper Image to buy clippers for my *nose* hair. There I was, talking to the guy about different nose hair trimmers. He looked at me with a zealous pitchman's smile and said, "This will trim nose *and* ear hair." My God, I thought, science has come through again. Then he handed me a contraption that looked like a weed-whacker for a Ken doll, and smiled. "This baby is waterproof. Perfect for those moments when you feel like sprucing up your nostrils while scuba diving."

Now I have four nose/ear trimmers, one for any situation. This guy was a good salesman.

Will scientists ever find a cure for ear or nose hair? I don't think so. First they have to figure out if we're really even here. Until that's settled, extraneous facial hair is sort of inconsequential. Anyway, I read somewhere that hair grows until you reach 40, then it goes in the opposite direction, into the head, and out the ears, nose, and other odd places. You think you're going bald, but it's not so. It's just growing on the inside. Is that at all a comfort to anyone? I didn't think so.

Women, of course, have grooming issues but also have mountains of help. They can choose from acres of cosmetics in department stores, as well as numerous plucking and curling devices. And they can visit the weird "facial" lady. I understand men are moving toward better personal care, and I'd like to move with them, but when I took advantage of a gift certificate I got for a facial, I almost landed another jail term for beating up the attendant. I think I was in the right. During the extracting process, she forced the dirt from my pores without my permission — and boy was my face red.

At work, I'm fortunate that I have stylists and makeup people to take care of my grooming issues. Even though I'm a manly man among men, I have no problem with all this personal attention. Believe me, a man who wears makeup every day doesn't have much of a line left to cross. So I've watched, listened, and learned. For instance, you can cover up blotchy skin and other bar-fight bruises with something called "foundation." This is not to be confused with the basis of an idea, an undergarment, or the stuff that holds up a house. Put any of those on your face and you're asking for trouble.

Sometimes I even go out in public with my makeup still on. But only when I am wearing pumps. Once, I went to a party and a strange woman looked at me and said, "My, are you pretty."

I knew exactly what she meant. I had on eyeliner and something to erase the bags beneath my lower lids. But she'd had one scotch too many, so you'll understand why I tried my best to be gracious. "Are you talking to me or to the bartender?"

"You. You're very pretty."

"You mean handsome, right?"

"No."

"I don't want to hear that, okay?"

At least now I know the effect Michael Jackson goes for. Sometimes he wants to be pretty, and in just the right light he looks a lot like my grandmother.

*

I THINK I'LL CLEAN UP the office now, and then work on the car. This room is always such a mess. The only thing the least bit orderly is the back wall bookcase. On the top shelf are the elements from *Home Improvement* that I've taken home over the years. Things that are very important for me to keep. Items I wanted to have because I love the show so much. Stuff I shamelessly pilfered from the set. One is a two-cycle impact wrench. We attached it to a two-cycle motor, so it actually worked. Hysterical. Blew it up.

I also have a couple mockups of sets that we built, that I took from the set designer. Should he want them back . . . I don't really know where I put them.

Oh, and if the Props department is still looking for that antique brass doorknob, it's here. Don't know how it got here, and I'll deny any involvement, but it's here. There's also a Buzz Lightyear doll, and other one-of-a-kind memorabilia I've collected.

The second shelf is full of car magazines I liked enough to keep. They are very expensive and printed on beautiful heavyweight paper. They're good for catching dust for at least ten years.

On the third shelf are all the *Home Improvement* scripts. Printed on a cheap copy bond, but timeless nonetheless.

The floor is covered with boxes full of more ancient memories. Whenever I open them, the past overwhelms me. Last time I looked through this stuff I found a tile from the first comedy club I ever played. I don't mean one of those hot plate trivets that you get at Niagara Falls. A regular tile. I chipped it out of the floor right in front of the bar, wrote my name on it, and framed it. No one tried to stop me; maybe they figured that anyone crazy enough to rip off a tile with a bunch of drunks watching was probably also armed and dangerous. By the way, I did a great set that night and I still don't understand why they've never asked me back.

Come to think of it, I thought I put that tile on the bookcase. It's not there. Now where did I put it? It should be on the shelf next to the water heater I took from the second club I played. I'm certain the urinal I borrowed from the third club is in the garage. That tile means a lot to me. It took me almost half an hour to chisel it out of the floor. Maybe I'd better look through these boxes again.

Here's one with all my old newspaper clippings. I collect way too much of what's been written about me because I figure one day I'll sit in front of the fireplace with boxes of stuff and say, "God, I remember that." Or, "I must be the world's biggest egotist."

What happened to that tile? I'd hate myself if I've lost it. I sense a pattern here. Three weeks ago I realized I'd lost an art portfolio that's very important to me. It's 20 years old and contains some of my earliest drawings. Things keep slipping through the cracks in my life. Next thing I know I'll hear voices calling to me from the other side.

I've got to find that tile. Maybe in this box. No, this is just old snapshots. Wow, here's one of me. God, how young I looked. So hopeful and ready to take on the world. Oddly, this changes my mood. Now, instead of feeling sad at how the years have passed, I realize something nice: I *have* succeeded in life. Why? Because I set goals.

I remember when I sent my first tape to Johnny Carson. I thought I was ready. An impetuous youth. But it was a goal worth pursuing. I believe setting goals is very important. Amidst the confusion I had a plan and, I know now, I was one of the lucky ones who made it work. (I also got a picture of myself and Johnny, which — between you and me — was really all I wanted.) That night, after the show, I wrote down three pages of goals: What I Want To Do In My Life. I probably shouldn't say any more about them, though, since I think the first was "Become Dictator of the Earth."

I learned about goals from a speaker in prison. He said that the best arrow in the world is no good unless it's directed someplace. He said something about the rings on a target, and how being "on-target," in Greek, meant "without sin." At least angle toward goodness, he said, and you'll achieve your goals. Later, I discovered that it all has to do with being positive instead of negative, with creating the universe instead of destroying it.

Maybe I'm not just an egotist. Maybe I was supposed to keep these memories because one day, when the time was right, I'd look through my boxes and understand that not only had I come a long way, but that it's time to set new goals.

That's nice. What's also nice is that the old picture reminds me where the tile is. It was framed, so I put it in a carton of pictures to be hung. A little heavy lifting and shifting and there's the box . . . and the tile.

Underneath the missing tile is another memory that means a lot. Was this little journey all about finding it? Did the tile just lead me here? I took this picture when I was in college. It was one of the last times I saw my friend Steven. We were dumping some wood one weekend, when we got his truck stuck in a muddy gully in the middle of nowhere, far from the road. We tried to get it out for hours and were about to spend the night in the great Michigan outdoors when this other car pulled close, almost as if I'd wished them there. We were saved by what we later came to believe were two angels. A young guy and girl — not related, they said — who looked like twins. They wore jean jackets and flannel shirts and were the gentlest people you'd ever meet. They *just happened to have* a towing chain in their trunk. They gave us ice cold drinks — but had no cooler in their car. We don't even know how they saw us in the gully since it wasn't visible from the road. Afterward, I took a picture of them with Steven.

Now, looking at the picture, Steven is sharply in focus, but the "angels" have faded. Wow. This blows my mind. Maybe they *were* angels. I turn over the frame to see if there's a rip in the backing paper that could cause this distortion, but it's still intact. Then I see the framer's little label on the bottom right corner. It reads: Penari's. Now where do I know that word from?

*

I N THE MIDDLE of this strange memory the doorbell rings and startles me. Am I expecting anyone? Maybe it's the plumber — no, that's this afternoon. If he even shows up. Maybe it's the guy with the tile samples?

"Who is it?" I ask, pushing the gate intercom button.

"Federal Express."

"Okay, c'mon in, Robert." Robert is my regular FedEx guy.

When I get to the front door, he's waiting on the steps. But it's not Robert. It's a young guy, handsome, maybe 25. He looks vaguely familiar. But how could I know him? He's not my regular guy. He smiles cheerily and hands me a FedEx box . . . addressed to my wife.

"Thanks."

"No problem," he answers. "Have a nice day."

"You don't mind working on Saturday?" I say, before he can turn to leave.

"I'm a goal-oriented guy, sir."

"Must be tough. So many other things to do."

"Nah, not for me. That means I get Mondays off. I like Mondays off. It's a goal I had a long time ago, to take Mondays off."

"Why Mondays?"

"Well, shopping is easier. Most stores are crowded on Saturdays and closed on Sundays."

"And that was a goal?"

"Yeah, a goal. I set my own. It's tough to set goals, but I think it's helpful."

"So you like your job."

"Yeah, I love my job," he says, with a twinkle in his eye. "I always wanted to work for Federal Express."

"One of your . . . goals?" He was saying what I'd just been thinking.

"I always think you should set goals. Don't you think it's a good idea to set goals?"

"In fact, I do," I say, while trying to read his name tag. We've talked long enough that I really should call him something other than, "uh huh." But when I try to read the name plate, the daylight around him begins to shimmer and brighten. It's hard to focus and I'm getting dizzy.

"You weren't hiding in my office a few minutes ago, were you?" I ask before I can stop myself.

"Of course not," he says, nonchalantly. "Anyway, sir. Gotta go. Have a nice life."

What the . . . ? Did he say "life"?

A couple seconds later he's in his truck, pulling out of the driveway. Then he sticks his head out the window and says what sounds like, "You like turkey bologna sandwiches with potato chips, and haven't seen Steven in a long time, correct?"

What the hell was that all about? Where did that guy come from? I've never seen him before. And why was he talking about goals? This is too weird. It's nuts. Laura was right. Quit reading weird books. Do something constructive. The Celebrity Wheels people will be here early on Monday. I've got to finish the hot rod and put on the hood ornament. If I can find it.

THREE

I HAVE THE GARAGE I've always wanted. There's room for four cars and a huge workshop. The garage is where men work with their hands and that's a beautiful thing. Women often say that nothing turns them on more than a guy who can create with his hands; that and money, power, jewelry, and money. And a sense of humor.

For me, the garage is a sanctuary far from the rules and restrictions that exist in the rest of the house. It's a place I can express my inner self, or simply express some of the natural noises my body makes without worrying about offending anyone.

This place is also a creative center. Some of today's greatest companies began in the garage. The Ford Motor Company, Delta Airlines, Apple Computers, and more than a few great rock-and-roll bands. There's something spiritual about the place. Maybe it's the size of the door, or all the machines inside. Maybe it's the work area or the tools or the smell of grease. It's not polished. There's no style, no pretense. It's all bare rafters and studs, and dirt in the corners.

Traditionally, the garage is where the cars live and, perhaps, even talk among themselves at night. Otherwise, the place is what you make it. It is what it is.

As a kid, I loved our old garage. It stood apart from the house. It was cold in the winter, stifling in the summer. The rafters were piled with junk. My current garage is part of the house, and though more modern and spacious, and a lot cleaner, it's still the home of function and maintenance.

And it's all mine. Well, Laura keeps her car in "my" garage, but *I* picked the car. Otherwise she doesn't venture in here except to do to me in my space what I do to her in her space, which is the rest of the house: She leaves shit around. So what if I stack piles of papers and books and folders everywhere — must Laura put boxes on my workbench? I've told her more than once that's not what my workbench is for. I mean, what if the fellas just dropped by one summer afternoon? How would I explain the clutter?

"Just got out the Christmas ornaments early, guys. Doesn't hurt to be prepared."

"Well, you're not really *using* your workbench," she always says. I think this is just her way of showing how disappointed she is that I don't do more with my hands. But even if I'm not in here enough, does that mean she gets to use my work bench as a trash receptacle? I don't think so. Besides, the garage is the one place I'm always cleaning and sweeping up. I know there's one way to make sure my territory is solely mine, but I don't want to have to pee on my work bench to prove it.

I don't expect we'll ever settle this issue. It's just another example of how men and women differ. We're different species, really.

My garage is my monument to manliness. I've got my phone out here, my black and white TV, and the tools I could use to do just about anything. I say "could" because Laura's right: I'm so busy now that the most important tool I have is the Yellow Pages. But like I said, there's nothing wrong with wanting to be ready just in case.

I've also got some pretty weird stuff in here. For instance, the

Visible Man and Visible Woman models. I bought them to build with my daughter, Kady, who lately insists that I call her Belle. (Those Disney movies!) No sooner had I got them home than I realized I'd actually have to paint all the internal organs by myself because Kady, oops — Belle — was only 13 months old and could barely find her mouth with a spoon, to say nothing of finding a plastic spleen the size of an already-chewed piece of gum, with a paint brush. Then I discovered I'd need 61 little bottles of Testor paint, Superman's acute eyesight, and full oxygen gear to keep from passing out from the smell. Naturally I was intrigued. Men love that sort of challenge.

These visible "people" make me a bit uncomfortable, though. Transparent skin, eyeballs just sitting in the sockets, and you can see what they had for lunch. If we really looked like that it would put doctors out of business.

"My side hurts, honey."

"Oh, look! There's your problem, right there. That thing's all inflamed. You've got a gall stone the size of a penny-loafer."

Naturally, the Visible Man and Visible Woman live in separate boxes, but one morning I came in early and found them in the same box. Now there are a couple little Visible Kids running around everywhere, and I had to buy a rare Visible Au Pair. I think there was some hanky-panky between the au pair and the dad because she suddenly moved away and now the parents don't speak to each other. They haven't shared a box in three years.

What else? I've got a remote-controlled car, a serious off-road racer. It's a clear plastic-body Toyota pickup truck. It took me the better part of a day to put the thing together. I spent several hours on the shock absorbers alone. "Tim the dad" had to build this so that "Tim the kid" could play with it. When it was finished I couldn't wait to show it to my wife, so I drove it across her, in bed, at three a.m. Boy, was she impressed.

My real hot rod looks even more wonderful. I'm glad to have this weekend alone to finally finish it. Goals are good, right? Better set the mood for work. I'll put on the TV: okay, a mud bog challenge, men. Hell, if it's got a motor, shit, we'll race it. I'm glad I put cable in the garage.

*

THERE'S JUST A FEW THINGS that need doing on the car: gap the spark plugs, fix the windshield post, put on the hood ornament — if I could just remember where I put it. But my mind is a blank. Oh, well, I'll just get busy on the other stuff and maybe it will come to me while I work.

According to most Eastern religions, the moment when a much-sought idea or answer finally pops into your head is a sudden, immediate insight.

Apparently, Buddhists do it all the time. But they would. See, they think that the original nature of man is that of the Buddha — which is the unity underlying everything. Only we, who are all manifestations of the Buddha (not different from the Buddha, but more like little nodes who think we're separate), have forgotten it. Here's another way to look at it: The Earth is alive, and we evolved *from* it. Yet we all think (or at least act) like we came here from someplace else. Like Pluto.

Of course, the Buddhists are trying to remember more than where they put the ceremonial tea set. To them the whole idea of life is to remember who we are, which is God. That instant of remembering is supposed to change you forever, and then you can finish brushing your teeth, use some salve on sore muscles, and go to bed.

Okay. Here's another interesting theory: Jokes are also an example of spontaneous intuitive insight. Supposedly in the moment you understand a joke and laugh, you experience enlightenment. And, of course, it has to be spontaneous because it's no good having to explain the joke.

So experience this: A guy walks up to his front door one night, sees a snail on the steps, and kicks it into the bushes. Three years later he hears a knock on the door. It's the snail. The guy looks down, the snail looks up, and says: "What the hell was that all about?"

Did you experience the enlightenment? Don't tell me I have to explain it to you, too.

Here's how a friend explained laughter to me over dinner one night. He said that laughter is a common denominator of the enlightened among us. "The American Indians acknowledge the spiritual aspect of laughter," he said. All big ceremonies were preceded by stand-ups. They called them Heyeohkas. (Pronounced: Hey-o-keys. The spelling is bizarre, but what do you want — they wrote on deerskin.) They used to swim in mud puddles, shave their hair, jump around and cause laughter in the tribe. But why? What does laughter do that's so damn mystical?

"It loosens you up," I guessed.

"That's one way of putting it. But what I mean is that it puts you in the moment. And when you're in the moment you're completely non-judgmental, just noticing — witnessing — the way things are and the way they ought to be. Noticing the disparity between them causes laughter."

As I'm thinking about this, a magazine I must have left on a shelf above me drops on my head. It falls open to a page with a cartoon about two fish, in which one looks at the other and asks, "What's this ocean thing we keep hearing about?"

*

THERE. I'VE FINISHED everything but the ornament. I'd better look around. I've searched for nearly half an hour with no luck. I'd better keep looking because I've got to find that thing. But one thing I'll never forget is how I got the ornament. It's a pretty weird story, but it's true.

A few years ago a group of us went to a hot rod show and auto swap meet in Pasadena. We wandered around for a while, checking out the cars. I was looking for some parts to start an as-yet-to-be-determined project, which turned out to be my 1946 hot rod. Out of nowhere I heard a tinkling. Nice word, "tinkling." Not too masculine, but that's the only way to describe the sound. If it had been like bells or chimes I would have said so.

Then I heard the sound again. It seemed like it was right inside my head.

Then I heard the sound again, right in my ear. I looked over my shoulder at where I thought it had come from and I saw a bearded old man, wearing a fishing vest, looking right at me. He stood behind a display table, three or four rows away, and in front of a great old Chevy delivery van. He cocked his head to one side and I heard the tinkling again.

That's when I should have run away. Instead, I said to my friend Brian, a guy who can really build hot rods, "I'm gonna go look at the car parts over there."

"All right," he said. "I'll go check out the new Mustangs."

I pointed at the old man's table. "I'll be over there."

*

THE OLD MAN DIDN'T say anything about the noise and I didn't ask him. To tell you the truth, I was a little afraid. See, this *had* happened once before, some years ago, at a Renaissance Pleasure Faire.

The faire was alive with the sounds of lutes and other period instruments, the booming voices of actors reciting Shakespearean verse, and the braying of lambs and goats. Do you know that if you listen to any animal talk long enough that it will eventually recite Shakespeare, or the lyrics to *Louie Louie*?

Every sign read, "Ye Olde This" and "Ye Olde That." I was quaffing an ale and adjusting my bloomers and cape when I heard bells. Insistent bells. It was as if they were right behind me. I turned, ready to duck what I thought was a mime who had been annoying me the entire day, as mimes are trained to do. But there was no mime. Instead I saw a lady, dressed in 16th-century costume, ringing these tiny bells from across a crowded field. I followed the tinkling sound.

She was a tarot card reader. I entered her tent and she read my fortune. What she told me scared me so much I have ever since called the deck "terror cards." She said, "You are a very old soul. You have been through this many times. You will know the results of your karma much faster than others. It will be instant. When you hurt someone, a day later *you* will be hurt." She also told me that I'd once been a powerful, but badass, Egyptian something or other, and had failed many times to learn the important lesson about good and evil. Then she gave me the big news: This was my last chance to live life correctly. I had to believe her, otherwise the $100 I'd just forked over was as good as flushed down Ye Olde Andy Gumpe. It turned out that not only did her story explain my affection for Egyptian jewelry and, eventually, my time behind bars (Get this: I was busted the *next* day, and soon went to jail), but I finally understood why I'm the only one I know who's certain Moses looked nothing like Charlton Heston in *The Ten Commandments.*

I also had another question.

"How come everyone with a past life was always someone important back then?" I asked. "Don't simple foot soldiers and common house slaves get to come back? I mean, what about the guy who cleaned up the horse shit after Ben Hur's chariot race?"

"Don't be an idiot," she spat. "This is not the time for jokes." Sometimes that moment of enlightenment is not where you expect it to be.

Then she went on about Mort. Now, this wasn't Mort from down at the deli, but *morte.* Death. Apparently, the day number of my birthday corresponds to this tarot card. Fortunately, she explained that it didn't mean my actual demise — just yet — but the death of something and the rebirth of something else. "You're embarking on a very big step in your life," she said, then added, "but you already know this, don't you?"

Unfortunately, she couldn't be any more specific.

I thanked her and went home and right to bed. Well, actually Ye Olde Bed.

*

FROM THE LOOK on the old man's face, I could tell he somehow knew about my unsettling memory. He said, "Relax, the old Tim has died. Now you will have the best year of your life."

"Isn't it a little late?" I said, nervously, while wondering how he knew my name. "The year's almost up. This is November."

"Okay, then next year," he said, with a smile.

"Thanks," I said. "You don't have a deck of tarot cards in your pocket?"

"Not at all," he said. "But I am glad to see you."

I then realized how he knew my name. I was a well-known comic.

"But how do you know I'm going to have a great year? You're not trying to sell me something, are you?"

"Well, 1979 was one of your worst years, right?"

The year I'd gone to jail. "This is kind of silly, isn't it?" I said.

"Yes, it is kind of silly."

"Were you in the population? Do you know me from there?"

"Not exactly. It's just that sometimes I get these feelings." Then he told me about his psychic feelings and how they helped him find the old parts he sold. "That's how I know to go to the right swap meets," he explained. "For instance, if I'm looking for something specific, like the door handle or side view mirror of a '33 Buick, all I have to do is think hard enough and I'll end up finding it."

"I tried that with women when I was single," I said. "Didn't work."

"Of course not. They're not from around here." Then he leaned over and whispered, "They're from another planet."

I said nothing. Neither did he. I decided to look at his stuff, and that's when something flashed in my eye, momentarily blinding me. It was a beam of sunlight reflecting off something at the far right end of the table. I followed it and discovered a small collection of old hood ornaments. Nowadays, most cars don't have them, but they used to, and some were quite ornate and impressive. The old man had five or six.

And that's when I saw it.

The ornament was beautiful and unlike anything I'd ever seen before. I couldn't stop looking at it. The craftsmanship was exquisite. It was some sort of graceful prehistoric bird with a predator's beak and its wings swept back, as if it had been frozen in time just as it was about to fly away. It seemed to contain within its lithe lines the possibility that it could at any moment break free and soar upwards. It was hard to believe the thing was made of . . . what *was* this metal?

The bird was mounted on an art deco base of stepped crystal. Little pieces of malachite formed a breastplate, in the center of which was a marking that looked like a small "t."

The sunlight danced on the crystal, throwing rainbow patterns across my eyes, and I thought I heard the tinkling in the wind once again.

I picked up the ornament and instantly felt a strange, warm, tingling sensation. For seconds I floated in a web of pure pulsating energy. I *was* pure energy. The ornament and I were one object composed of billions of atoms present at the Big Bang.

Suddenly, my fingertips were on fire and I knew something magical had happened. As it turned out, my fingertips were burning because the ornament was red hot from sitting in the sun all afternoon. No matter. I had to own it.

I could start building my dream hot rod by buying the final part first. The ornament would be the catalyst, the last piece of the puzzle. The old man must have read my mind.

"Ten dollars," he said.

I paid him and walked off with my prize.

*

N OW I HAVE no idea where the ornament is. That doesn't mean I can't take pleasure in searching, if only because searching is a process, and process is what life's all about. We always hear that it's best to enjoy the ride, and not just arriving, because we actually spend most of our lives "getting there."

One process I love is building cars. I've always liked them. My dad loved them. He was forever monkeying around under the hood and chassis. The great thing is that I came about my passion for cars honestly. My dad never tried to shove his love of cars down my throat — which is a good thing since I'm sure that would have required extensive surgery.

My dad managed to remodel every automobile we had. My parents would buy a car — a fine 1961 Ford family wagon, for instance — and right out of the box he'd put on a high-rise manifold, dual exhausts, and glass packs. His modifications to the family vehicles weren't always major, but it was enough to qualify him as my kind of guy, rewiring everything, giving it more power. I don't even know where he did this stuff, or when he had the time. He had a green Volkswagen, of all things. This was his hot rod. He loved that car, modified the motor, and waxed and polished it all the time. When he did this he was happy and balanced, and when I watched him, I was, too.

I've always loved stuff that moved and that could take me places. When I got my first bike, I think my development was pretty much arrested right then and there. That was enough, and I was happy. Cars came next, and when I got my driver's license, the kid in me was thrilled, and the neighborhood was in jeopardy.

Some people consider cars as transportation only. For others they're a statement of style. Mostly I meet people who want to buy a very functional piece of equipment, but don't know why they want the one they want. They ask me what they should get. But when I tell them, they go, "Nah, I don't want it." And thank you for asking.

Some people believe you can tell a lot about a guy by the car he drives. Is that the same for a woman, or would those people suggest it's the washing machine she owns?

So what can you say about the guy who drives a gray Honda Accord? Practical? A guy with a red Accord is practical but he wants to pretend he's a little naughty. Red Accord with mag wheels? He wishes it was a BMW, but it's about as close as he can get, leaving him slightly bitter. Red Accord with mag wheels and a Chevy 427 engine wedged in under the hood? You've got a guy with some serious issues.

Here's another thing I want to know: Why do so many people who don't really use them buy 4-wheel drive sports-utility vehicles? If you're not actually working for the phone company or the power company — that's a utility — what's the point? I think they might be compensating for a height problem. This is another example of buying a car for style and image.

I buy a car for function: that is, doing what it does best. What's important is how it drives. Like a Ferrari, for instance. Now, I'm not saying the fact that it boasts that fine Ferarri styling isn't a plus. It's icing on the cake. And boy, do the babes love it.

A great thing about cars is that they can forge deep bonds between you and men you might not otherwise like. There's a couple guys I talk to at my old gym back in Michigan. We have only one common interest: cars. When we talk about them, we're equals. We get excited. We one-up each other. We say, "Wouldn't it be great to do this?" "I'd love to have one of these." "Have you ever driven one of those?"

We don't talk about our wives this way. One reason is that no self-respecting guy is going to tell his pals, "Boy, is my wife hot in the sack." Not only is he betraying private stuff, but who needs other men sniffing around?

*

JUST THEN THE DOG saunters into the garage. Wait a second. How'd she open the door? It doesn't push in. When you're on the other side, it has to be pulled. And I know I closed it. I suppose this is what happens because I don't spend enough time at home. Either the family teaches the pets strange tricks to drive me crazy and keep me on my toes, or the animals who live with me know much, much more than they're letting on. Occasionally I test her.

"Look Spot. If you *are* a shape-shifting alien of superior intelligence, here doing research, it must be hard on you when you have to sniff other dogs' behinds to keep up appearances. So just tell me. It's okay. It'll be our little secret, I swear."

She responds by lifting her eyebrows and wagging her tail furiously, as if she's just aching for me to pet her. What an incredibly sweet dog. Or possibly a brilliant alien actress.

So I welcome Spot. She is the only female I enjoy hanging around with in the garage. I even have a picture of her on the pegboard. She likes to come in, lay down, and sleep. She's also the only female I know who can get comfortable curled up on the concrete floor without whining.

Just for fun, I ask Spot if *she* knows where the hood ornament is. No answer. That's okay.

And then it hits me that maybe I'm happy about not finding the hood ornament. It keeps the process of building the car alive. To actually finish the car might depress me. Then what would I do?

I wonder if Kady took the hood ornament? I just noticed that her bike's in the garage. It's not supposed to be in here. Maybe she *did*. I'll have to search her room.

I'm halfway through the door to the house when the phone rings. Well, no need to trip on the steps, running into the kitchen to grab it before the machine answers. I've got that handy garage extension!

"What!"

"Hel . . . T . . . m."

"What?"

" . . . t's . . . L . . . r. We're a . . . the . . . "

"I can't hear you. You're breaking up."

Then the phone goes dead. And rings again.

"Tim." It's Laura.

"Where are you?"

"At the ca . . . site. Can yo . . . h . . . me?"

"The connection's really bad," I say. "Everything okay?"

"Ye . . . I . . . n . . . hear yo . . ."

"I hate cell phones. Just say hi to Kady. I love you."

"L . . . y . . . too."

"Oh, wait. You haven't seen the hot rod hood ornament, have you? They're coming to get the car Monday morning and I've got to find it."

"Wher . . . the wh . . . t . . . ?

"What? It's where? You're breaking up. Call later. I love you."

Guess I've got to search the house.

FOUR

KADY'S ROOM IS her private world. I'm rarely in here alone. It feels kind of weird, almost intrusive, to stand here looking around. The place smells like her, feels like her, and reflects her individuality. Since she's my daughter, we of course share traits and habits and features, but even so, as each day passes it is sometimes hard to believe she's actually a part of me. She is, as I figure all moms and dads one day realize, more than the sum of her parents' parts. She is us, yet she is something entirely new.

Kady was a baby in this room, and I can still feel those memories. But in a deeper sense, this is now uncharted territory, another world, a different planet.

It's a girl's room.

It's full of much I don't understand. But one thing is certain: I wouldn't change a thing.

No, I lied. I wish she'd put her stuff away.

*

LIKE MOST MODERN DADS, I was in the delivery room when my daughter was born. My first instinct was to run away. I wanted to pack fast, leave quickly, and never come back. I thought about heading for South Carolina, buying a hardware store, and starting a new life. The authorities probably would have caught up with me, though, since I planned on calling the store "Tim Allen's Home Improvement."

Before Kady was born, I didn't think having a kid would be such a big deal. My attitude was simple: Babies are nice, play with them, put them in the closet until the next time. Then my daughter arrived, all pink, wrinkled, and crying, and I suddenly realized I had a big responsibility. I was scared. I admit it. Marriage is one thing, but a kid? What an ... an ... er ... ah ... anchor.

Of course, I didn't run. I couldn't. I was frozen in place. Laura had been squeezing my hand so hard during the final push that we were still locked tight. Actually, I think she was holding on for more reasons than just the pain factor. She knows me. Fight or flight. Also, the doctor must have seen the look on my face because she later thanked me for not getting physically ill in her delivery room.

Most guys supposedly get afraid *during* pregnancy. This occurs just about the time the wife's cute little tummy expands to the size of a regulation basketball. For the dad-to-be it's the shock of the real, and he is gripped by the certainty that he's made a big mistake going along with the "my biological clock is ticking, it's time to have a kid" thing. He envisions his carefully constructed "couple" life in ruins. Maybe it's the color draining from his face, or his sudden need to spend more time with the guys on weekend camping trips, but eventually the mom-to-be notices in her sweet way.

"What's with the weird face?"

"Nothing."

"I can see something's wrong."

"You're right. It's the, uh, b . . . b . . . "

"You don't want me to breast feed?"

"No, no . . . "

"Is it the diapers? I thought you *wanted* to use a diaper service instead of polluting the environment."

"Not that."

"Then what?"

"It's just . . . it's . . . , do you think we're doing the right thing? I mean, now that I think about it, maybe we should have waited to start a family."

This is when she touches her midsection, smiles with clenched teeth and, fighting for control, says, "Maybe you should sleep at your office tonight."

Guys know the look. Time for a hasty retreat. "Aw, honey, of course I want the baby. I, uh, just wanted to make sure *you* wanted the baby."

Then the baby arrives and everything changes. The new dad falls so hard for his innocent newborn that he could tie a bow around his bursting heart and sell it for Christmas. He proclaims to all who will listen, and many who would rather not, that the baby changed his life. Being a dad is great. He urges all his male friends to have kids as soon as possible, though he's careful to remind the single ones to get married first. Meanwhile, Mom glows and nods approvingly. It's heartwarming. And insufferable. We knew some couples like that. We don't see them anymore.

For me, the time before Laura got pregnant was great. I thought she was so damn fine. We spent many hours, er . . . alone, getting to know each other intimately. Then Laura gave me the news: She was with child. Considering how much fun we were having, I think that was God's way of saying, "ENOUGH ALREADY!"

My friends *were* right about one thing: The baby does destroy your previous life. Laura and I had perfected our routine: Work, travel, cocktail parties, travel, gifts to each other. It wasn't a bad way to live, except when she expected me to wear the chaps to bed. Then — it was even better. Yippee ki-o ki-ay.

Kady's birth broadened our lives by making us focus on another human being. In other words, the baby demanded lots of time and energy. What I really mean to say is that we signed a lifetime contract with no escape clause. At the time I believed that forsaking my own needs in the service of another was transforming. Now I think I was so sleep-deprived that I couldn't have been thinking clearly, and signed under extreme duress.

Looking back on the past few years I realize that the whole fatherhood experience has turned me into a different guy. Once, when an inconsolable infant cried nonstop on a plane, its wail penetrating my complimentary headset even though I was tuned to the in-flight John Philip Sousa Channel, I would think, "Look, I paid for the seat and I did *not* pay to have that kid screaming. Haven't you people heard of chloroform?"

But being a father has brought me smack into the family of man. I'm less judgmental. Now, my first thoughts are, "Maybe some chewing gum will help her ears. . . try some apple juice . . . can I do something? . . . maybe if I held her for a couple minutes . . . what's the matter with you people? . . . Just *give* the damn kid to me. I'll take care of her. Go get a cocktail and calm down!"

Having Kady made me both fiercely protective *and* softened me to life. She opened me up to hope. Kids are about hope. Kids are about the future. They're about *our* future. They're about having someone around we can guilt into taking care of us when our minds make appointments our bodies can't keep.

I like the guy I am *now* better than the guy I used to be.

*

THE GUY I USED TO BE is no longer here. Now, if only I could be sure that the guy I *am*, is. You know what I'm saying: Am I really here? The great 17th-century French mathematician and philosopher Rene Descartes also posed this question. His answer was: "Cogito ergo sum." In English, "I think, therefore I am." I don't have to think about that twice to agree. I must exist, or who'd be asking the question?

Sometimes I feel like there's a tiny, but quite handsome, man in my head running the Tim Dick/Tim Allen show. The problem with this is that if there is a tiny man in my head, there must be a tinier man in *his* head, and so on and so on and so on. No wonder I'm suffering from detachment, as well as a whopper of a headache?

That's the Western way of thinking. Eastern mystics say that there's no one home inside us, no "I" even asking the question. The "I," they claim, is an illusion. Okay, fine. So tell me smart guys: who's doing the looking?

Sometimes I think I shouldn't bother with any of this because we have but one moment in time and this chasing my philosophical tail is not exactly making the most of it. Besides, don't I "lose" myself every day? I think about physics, and suddenly Tim is gone. I do a scene for my show, and I'm gone. I have sex — gone. And yet I always come back. I reconstitute myself, or at least the history of my memories.

Unfortunately, none of these realizations has made a dent in my anxiety about what to expect from the universe, not to mention this year's Publisher's Clearing House sweepstakes. In fact, far from it. Here's what I mean: Say Descartes is right. I exist. Okay. I may be here, but you may *not* be. What if you're just a figment of my imagination? How can one tell the difference? And if that's not confusing enough, turn it around. You could be here, and I could be a figment of *your* imagination. (If this is the case, my congratulations.) What if all this is a dream, and not necessarily yours *or* mine? Maybe everything is part of the R.E.M. patterns of some homeless guy. Promise that if you see him you won't wake him up.

I've always wondered what happens if you stand Descartes' statement on its head. If "I think, therefore I am" is true, is the opposite also true: "I am, therefore I think"? Let's settle that issue right now: Hugh Grant. Michael Jackson. Joey Buttafuoco. Must I go on?

I have another question. What *is* thinking? A facet of consciousness? Of ego? Bad digestion? A chemical reaction in the brain? (Are they the same?) Is it "That which the mind does"? What is the mind, anyway? Where is it found? How do people lose it? We generally agree it's in the head, except when we want to insult someone and then we accuse them of having their mind in the gutter/between their legs/in their behinds.

Here's a thought: Perhaps consciousness is the face of the unity underlying everything that the mystics (and now the physicists) talk about. Maybe our minds are our connection with what the Hindus call the Brahman, the Buddhists call the Buddha, and the verifiably paranoid — or perceptive — call the Phone Company.

Some scientists even think there are two kinds of consciousnesses, a disembodied mind and an organic embodied mind, each with its own "spot" in the brain where they interphase. One is "local," the self-aware chemical reaction we call consciousness. The other is non-local, with a thought-speed connection to the universal consciousness. And unlike cable TV, all the premium channels are free.

In these books I read, all signs point to all things being interconnected. I can buy that, maybe. But then it goes further. Reality is not even supposed to be what we see immediately surrounding us, but in its deepest sense, reality is — again — the oneness we're all supposed to be a part of. Sounds sort of kooky, I know. All I know now — and I mean "know" in an intuitive, not an intellectual sense — is that something more than I can perceive is going on. I just feel it.

More on this when I complete my home study course in mental telepathy.

Tell you what, try this: First think of everything as energy. Then, if the "real" me is but a ripple in this energy, then my mind/thought/consciousness is perhaps a ripple of this ripple, occupying no space and no time, outside of these constraints, and it is now capable of time travel and being in two places at once. Think about it.

How about something simpler, like what you had for breakfast? Good. Now think about how cool you'd look in a new Ferrari. Yes. Now think of me as channeling an ancient scholar who needs funds. Great. Now write me a check for $100 and send it to me, care of the publisher. Boy, are you easy.

I do get excited chasing after the answers. This questioning is not only what can cause the malaise and the detachment, but what combats it. I feel like I did when I was a kid, always unearthing new, neat stuff. Every time I turn a page and find an unexpected way to look at the nature of existence, I think, "Wow." Sometimes I even say it out loud, though I try hard these days not to move my lips when I read . . .

This constant process of discovery is at the root of a strong connection between myself and my daughter. After all, discovery plays a huge role in her life. At her age, everything is new. She can be thrilled by new crayon colors. Frankly, those sparkly ones kind of give me goose bumps, too.

*

AFTER KADY WAS BORN, the first thing Laura and I had to get used to was having another person in the house.

Before starting the family, we had asked our friends for advice. One swore that the best way to find out if we could handle parenthood was to get a pet. We were a bit reluctant since the idea of a standard poodle in diapers, while certainly worth a chuckle, seemed not at all practical, to say nothing of problems down the line, like private schooling and driving privileges, and strangers speculating which parent the poodle favored. We were, however, almost convinced to get a pet, when this very same friend adopted a four-week-old kitten she found on her front step.

We decided to watch her and learn — and it's a good thing we did.

After two days, she got so tired of changing the cat box that she gave the kitty to a Mongolian couple on her block to use in a feline fondue.

The whole episode convinced us that babies are not at all like cats, dogs, turtles, birds, fish, or any pet. Babies need constant food and love and attention. Pets need that too, but you can probably get away with less. Also, babies can't use a catbox, and shredded newspaper on the floor becomes nothing but a choking hazard. And you can't just buy them off with a cheap treat and a biscuit — at least not until they're older. Perhaps worst of all, babies have no natural fur to keep them warm, so you can't kick them outside at night when they bother you by trying to sleep at the foot of the bed, or worse, on your head. Well, you can kick them out, but the guilt factor is tenfold. Then, all too soon, kids learn to walk and talk, and talk back. I'm big enough to admit there were times I've wondered if perhaps we should have gotten some Siamese fighting fish when we had the chance.

However, without Kady, our lives would be incomplete. The minute I carried her over the threshold, our house finally became a home. Actually, I carried Laura, who carried Kady, who looked so beautiful and innocent that I almost dropped them both, as well as Laura's luggage which, having no free hands, I had to hold in my teeth.

Now my little girl has her own room, full of her own stuff. What I hope is that somewhere in here I'll find something that is part of my stuff: the hood ornament.

*

I DON'T SEE the ornament anywhere — at least not in plain sight. However, there are dolls, horses, knickknacks, stuffed animals, art projects, colorful beads, and frilly things. Only women don't call it "frilly." They call it attractive.

As I poke around, what strikes me most is how cheesy toys are these days. They lack . . . quality. Just take a tour of your local Toys R Us and you'll see what I mean: Many modern toys are cheaply constructed and meant to be discarded and replaced in order to keep the big toy machine going. Planned Obsolescence. I used to think quality was wood over plastic. Now it's a fine, crafted plastic over thin, flimsy plastic.

According to Robert Pirsig in his book, *Zen and the Art of Motorcycle Maintenance*, "quality" is a quality we all recognize when we encounter it. But Pirsig wanted to go a step further and define it. That turned out to be a very difficult task. I think you'll agree that we all know *intuitively* what quality is, and that life would not be the same without "it," although the "it" or essence is, like Pirsig concluded, without definition.

The ornament isn't in this box, but there is a Slinky. (I wonder how *that* would look mounted on the hot rod?) Playing with it, I realize how little we grow. The casing gets older, but the meat inside remains the same. I've always thought of myself as frozen at 14 years old, a kid trying desperately to run a man's life and fit into his relaxed-fit jeans, and this moment just makes me believe it even more. As long as the kid stays intact within, I am whole.

*

KADY'S GOT decorative boxes everywhere. On shelves, in the closet, under the . . . bed.

Wow. So this is where she keeps all the faxes I've ever sent her when I've traveled. I once suggested to her she keep them, but I didn't realize she had. I'm moved. Too bad there aren't that many. Now I feel awful.

I have not been enough a part of this child's life.

I'm not an absentee dad. It's worse. I call myself CGI dad. CGI stands for Computer Graphic Imaging. It's the process we use to make special effects in the movies: The sled flying through the Christmas night in *The Santa Clause*. The dinosaurs in *Jurassic Park*. Oh my God, you . . . thought it was real? I feel terrible.

With computer graphics, we can make something that's not really there seem like it is there. As a CGI (Computer Generated Image) dad

I can eat, talk, give Kady a bath, read her a story, and much more, without actually being in the room.

Right now, of course, I'm in the room, but she's not here. Bad timing.

Don't misunderstand me. I love her very much. I love everything she touches, her little hands, her gestures. But I'm always so busy, my foot jammed on the gas pedal of life. Something important is always going on. Someone always needs my attention. Or I've got a project I want to do. I could be at work, or using my computer, or tinkering with my cars, or just vegging in front of the television. I've got enough guilt to last me my lifetime and yours.

Once, Kady said to me, "You've been watching TV all day." She was right. I got up about 9:30 in the morning, turned on the TV, and sat there doing my mail and my work the entire day, with the TV blaring in the background.

Laura has told me a million times to just get away from the computer, or to stop watching TV, and listen to my daughter.

"Talk to her. Go outside with her. Play with her."

"Yeah, yeah, as soon as I finish this. I will in a minute. Just a minute. Be right there." How many times have I said, "In a minute. All right, just give me a second." It always turns into a half hour, and Kady loses interest.

I'm making progress, though. I know that every minute I don't spend with her at this — or any — age is a minute I can't get back. I know that when my time comes I won't suddenly sit up on my deathbed and say, "Gee, I wish I'd spent more time at the office." I might wish I hadn't been so scrupulous with my expense account, but that's about the extent of it.

Before I can sink too deeply into self-pity, I open a jeweled box and find a photo of Kady and me. She's very small, and wearing a cute dress. We're walking and holding hands. The picture is taken from behind. We didn't even know we were being photographed. She's looking up at me. That was a time of life when my life was more my own. I miss it.

I'm really touched that she's kept this photo in her special place. It must mean a lot to her. I wonder what else is in this box? I can see something under the picture. It seems to be glittering. It's another picture. Of Yanni? His eyes were twinkling. Oh well, at least she finally got rid of that publicity still of Alan Thicke. Not that there's anything wrong with these guys — but in the same box? It's funny how the value you place on things adjusts when they're suddenly juxtaposed with something else.

*

I REALLY AM WORKING on developing more of a father-daughter relationship with Kady. It's just that she's a girl and I'm a boy and this is strange territory for me. I'm really at a disadvantage because I have yet to figure out what she likes.

For instance, she wasn't exactly thrilled by the rocks I brought home from Venezuela, after I got home from shooting my second film. I also tried to interest her in robots. She'd seen some at a toy fair and liked how they moved around on the ground. So I started a collection for her. Now the collection is mine. I should have known.

She didn't like the car or the gun collection I started for her either, and frankly, she doesn't seem to have much interest at all in the explosives.

I think I know the problem: None of these things are soft and kooshy. Robots' chests open up and guns come out and lights flicker. They make loud noises and she hates loud noises. Also, she can't style their hair. There's really not much to do with the robots except *feel their power.*

Kady does like to wrestle, though. And she likes to get really rough. Rougher than I expect a girl would be. I think it bothers her, like it would bother a little boy, that I'm stronger than she is. So she starts growling at me and gets really excited. Then she'll cheat. She doesn't like to get beat. I suppose I could let her win, but I don't. I figure she wouldn't believe her own victory, and it would be developmentally unsound. There I'd be, kicking her butt, and all of a sudden I roll over and let her win? Kids aren't stupid. When we're outside, she doesn't like that I can play ball better than she does, either. But that doesn't stop me from playing to win.

All right, come on. How would it look if I lost to a little girl 37 years my junior? I've got *some* pride.

The furthest I've reached into her girl's world was when I brought home pictures of unicorns. She saw *Fantasia* and liked the unicorns, so I got her an animation cell, which she loved. She's also smart enough to realize that it's a calculated move on my part. Fortunately, she let me save face and accepted my offering. Pretty little pictures are my bridge to her woman's soul. It's all I've got. I'm not really good at the Barbie thing.

Even though I've made some mistakes, there is an upside. Because of the robots, Kady is now very popular with little boys who come to visit and play. She has power they want. They go, "Wow! Robots!" Then they ignore her for the rest of the afternoon. That, too — the ignoring — will pass.

I can't explain this to her for another couple years, but I've always thought that if a woman wants a man to notice her, she should spend *all* her money on a nice car — for instance, a Corvette — even if she'd be happier driving a Hyundai. Guys will invariably take heed.

A kick-ass stereo system, fancy camera equipment, or powerful computer will also do. But just having them isn't enough. A woman has to know how to *use* what she's got and know the terminology, too.

For instance, she has to know that RAM is an acronym for "random access memory" and not some new after shave.

When I was a kid, a woman named DeLynn had a black Corvette. She was a little like a motorcycle chick and all the other women didn't like her, but she got around. She attracted a lot of attention. Probably not the right attention, but men did notice her.

With a sensible savings plan in place, Kady will one day be able to afford all the toys she wants. I know I could just give her this stuff, but that would hardly develop her sense of money's worth. So to help her get started down the road to fiscal responsibility, I bought her a top-of-the-line Macintosh Power PC loaded with the latest spreadsheet and financial analysis program. All she needs to do now is figure out how to carry the computer from my office to her bedroom and she's on her way.

Until then, we're teaching her that she has to earn her money by giving her a dollar-a-week allowance. To get it she has to help feed the pets, clear her dinner plate and take it to the sink, clean up her room, mend all my clothes, change the oil in the car, and take care of any minor medical emergencies around the house — out patient surgery — that sort of thing.

Then she divides her allowance into three home savings plan "canning" jars. The first is for Small Things, like candy and gum. The second is for Big Things, like a bicycle or liquor. The third is for Other People, meaning charity, and when I need gas money.

*

I'D LIKE TO SPEND more time not only with Kady but with the whole family. One thing I still dream of accomplishing is to go out in public and be a little bit more like normal people. Yeah. Fat chance. I'm not complaining about being famous, of course, but I *have* observed how difficult it can be. I can barely take the family to a motion picture. When we went to Disneyland, they put us on all the rides by ourselves: There we were, a pathetic little man and his family, riding along, going, "Wheee! Woo-whoo!! That's fun."

"How did you like that, Mr. Allen?"

"Oh, that's terrific."

It's a little embarrassing to be screaming all by yourself on Mad Hatter's spinning teacups.

I once tried to take Kady to a water park. I don't think we can do it again unless I rent out the entire place for the afternoon.

Everybody brought their little kids over: "We love *The Santa Clause*." "We love *Toy Story*." "We love *Home Improvement*." I'm thrilled they do, believe me, but when it means I can't keep an eye on my daughter in a big crowd, it gets a little scary.

Being a dad has taught me patience, though. The boy in me and the girl in Kady fight a lot. She's very bossy. I am, too. The little boy in me doesn't tolerate that attitude from anyone, and never did. I think it's simple physics. If something is pushed, it will most likely push back. No, make that schoolyard physics.

Conventional wisdom says that being a parent and being a friend to your kids are at cross-purposes. You have to choose, and the right choice is parent. You have to draw lines, or the kid will be a messed up adult. But be fair. Too strict or too lax are both dangerous. I'd like to be friends, and in a way we are, but sometimes I have to tell Kady to just do what I say.

"I'm not telling you these things because I hate you," I explain. I heard this same reason a million times from my mother. "I'm not doing this because I'm an angry parent. I'm not doing this because I don't value who you are. It's because I know more than you about this matter, and to save some time and some wear and tear on your little psyche." Actually, that's how I wish my mom had put it. What she really said was, "If you don't listen right this minute, there's going to be some wear and tear on your butt when your father gets home."

I suppose I could do that, but at the moment Kady is going through a classic six-year-old phase where she says, "You're not the boss of me. I'm the boss of myself."

I could threaten her, but I've developed a new approach.

"Oh, yeah? Well, boss, why don't you run down to the store and grab me a six-pack. And while you're at it, wash the car and detail it. I don't want any Armor All on the tires, though."

"But Daddy, I can't drive."

"Gee, that's tough. The boss can't drive?"

Kady also likes to turn her ice cream into soup. When I was a boy, doing that made my dad angry. He'd take the bowl away and say, "You either eat ice cream or I'll fix you soup."

"But Dad, soup is salty with vegetables in it," I'd say. "I don't get the connection." Even then, a comedian.

I think what he really hated was the noise of the spoon clanging against the side of the bowl as his boys tried to turn good ice cream into mush, and he is trying to watch TV.

The first time Kady did this I said, "Eat the ice cream or I'll fix you sooooouu . . . " It was odd, as if I was channeling my dad. Then I realized I didn't care what she did to the ice cream. I like soft ice cream; I still like playing with it. So why make a big deal out of it? By not saying anything I broke the behavior chain. Years from now Kady will probably ask her kids, "What's wrong with you? Why don't you just stir it into a soup?"

And they'll say, "Yuck. Mom. It's ice cream. Soup is salty and has vegetables in it."

*

I WONDER HOW my daughter will grow up.

Not too long ago, she met Katy Coleman and Katherine Thornton, two astronauts, one of whom has walked in space. (I understand the other skipped, or played hopscotch, or something.) They go to schools and talk to the kids. It's very encouraging for young girls to see two women doing a job that was once the exclusive domain of men. Katy Coleman told my daughter to aim high for the stars and think of good things to do. It really opened her horizons. I asked her if she wanted to be an astronaut, too. She said no. She wants to be a policeman or fireman because she thinks it will be too tough to wash her hair in space. That's my girl!

I want Kady to be anything she wants to be. However, it would be okay if she grew up to be like Candice Bergen, the daughter of the really cool Edgar Bergen. I'd consider that a beautiful reflection and continuation of what I do best, which is make people laugh. She could also be a funny astronaut, fireman, or policeman, and I'd be happy.

The bottom line for me is that we love each other. It's so natural. The most important thing I've discovered is that I love her best when I'm not scared of her, when I'm not worrying myself crazy because she's a girl and I'm a boy and I don't understand all there is to understand about her, or because I'm afraid I haven't been a good enough dad. Fear gets in the way of love, and I've discovered that fear, and not hate, is the opposite of love. Think about it: Love and hate are closely bound emotions, but cousins, not enemies. It's fear that kills love. It's fear we feel when love is threatened.

When I think of this in terms of all the physics and metaphysics I've been plowing through and trying to understand, it seems to me that love is the closest the human mind has come to describing — intellectually — the unity that we're all searching for.

Every time I worry about me and Kady I'll have to remember that.

*

E VEN THOUGH I think I could do better in some parenting departments, and sometimes question how good a dad I really am, Kady and I do have special moments when we're so much a part of one another, words cannot describe it. This usually happens when I get the chance to put her to bed and tell her a story about when I was a little boy. For some reason she likes me to rub her hands and feet while I do this. Then she puts her arm on me to make sure I don't sneak out while she's falling asleep.

Once, while Kady was drifting off, that picture of the little girl who died in the arms of the fireman after the Oklahoma City bomb blast flashed into my head and I just started sobbing — so loud I thought I might wake her up. I generally don't cry, but sitting there, holding her hand, all I could think about were *that* little girl's parents, and then about parents all over the world whose kids had died as the result of violence in its many forms. I knew at that moment how much my daughter just being here reinforces my respect for life.

In fact, I'm thinking about Kady's hands right now. Little hands that might have put my hood ornament somewhere I'll never find it.

*

WHERE ELSE IN HERE can I look for this missing car part? All that's left is the closet. I've avoided it so far because to me it's like a larger-than-life version of a woman's purse. I know better than to go into a woman's handbag, so the idea of looking in a female's closet just scares the hell out of me. Laura and I have separate closets. She's got the big walk-in, in the bedroom, and I have a converted old linen closet in the hall. I've peeked inside the door to Laura's closet, but I swear I've never actually gone inside. I might not make it out. Once, when she asked me to find a particular purse, I had to call my neighbor's wife to come over and help me.

When I open the door, I almost jump out of my skin. Kady's closet looks just like . . . Laura's closet, only the clothes are smaller and neatly arranged on smaller hangers. There's no mistaking whose daughter she is. I see the pair of *Wizard of Oz* Dorothy slippers I bought her. I recognize a dress I purchased while I was filming *The Santa Clause*. (It was too small for me, so I reluctantly gave it to Kady.) It was a beautiful dress and she wore it all the time, until it got "too bunchy." One day, when we're about the same age, I'll ask her what that means. Anyway, now the dress hangs there looking so tiny that I'm instantly struck by how quickly she's grown.

Like her mother, Kady also has lots of shoes. Some have never been worn. I guess this means I shouldn't buy a little girl tennis shoes with cleats, or Italian leather driving shoes.

Even so, Kady does take after me in the *way* she wears her

clothes. If I find something I like, I'll wear it out. I had a yellow shirt once that my wife made the mistake of complimenting me on. Then one day, after wearing it 45 times in a row, she said it didn't look all that good anymore. I was confused. "I thought this was the one you liked!"

"Tim, look in the mirror. There's a stain on the front, the stitching's coming out, and the collar has pilled." She stared for a moment. "Oh, was that the yellow one?"

Apparently, clothes have an evolution as well, and when you've grown to love a garment, like I have this old friend, I guess you just don't notice it growing old. However, the pilling thing really caught me off guard. Now I'm afraid to wear it again, though unbeknownst to my wife, I did not get rid of the shirt. I buried it in a closet. It's the part of my closet with all the shirts that are too old to wear, but that I still love.

Suddenly I feel like someone's staring at me. I don't see the cat or dog either. Am I cracking under the midlife strain? No. This feeling's coming from somewhere. Then I realize it's Kady's dolls.

Like any little girl, she has dolls all over her room. There are so many you hardly notice them. Most of the dolls are pretty cool, but she's got one collection that she calls "fragile dolls." If you've seen enough Gothic fright flicks you'll know what I mean. Remember all those up-angle shots of catatonic, porcelain faces that have witnessed an unspeakable horror but, being dolls without the pull-strings in back, can't say anything? Their little, all-too-human eyes make me feel like an intruder. They've hemmed me in. I feel a bit faint and . . . wait: I swear to God the one in the middle was not there before. They'd better not be moving and switching places when I'm not looking, or I'm going to have to rent a hotel room for the weekend. No, I definitely don't remember that little redheaded number sitting in the center, with her arm around the teddy bear. And how come that doll on the far right looks like this morning's FedEx guy?

I've definitely overstayed my welcome here. I've searched all I can. I could still look through her chest of drawers, but as far as I'm concerned, if the ornament is in this room then I will have to wait to find it until we remodel or move out.

Now something's scratching at Kady's door. It better not any of that doll's friends. I'll crack it open an inch and peek out. Hey, it's Spot and she's got something in her mouth. It's a videocassette.

Since when does Spot watch movies?

FIVE

AT LEAST SPOT has excellent taste. The videotape in her mouth, now sticky with dog saliva, is what's left of my copy of *The Santa Clause*.

The Christmas it came out was very special. My first film was a success, the family had a great holiday, and the highlight was my younger brother's video tape of our family Christmas gathering at my Mom's house. He also took her film reels of Christmases past, transferred them to video, added a few sentimental scenes and edited them all into a nice holiday keepsake. Not only is this cassette a sentimental record of cherished memories, it's also a helpful visual reminder to those who had such a good time celebrating that they have no memory of anything at all. It will come in handy in case anyone tries to sue.

I am glad Spot decided on *The Santa Clause*, and not a special family tape to snack on. I guess she didn't see Yanni's video concert in the cabinet. Maybe she's hungry.

A big bone will have to do.

"How about a treat?" I ask. Spot wags her tail excitedly and runs into the utility room, where we keep her dog bones. She loves those dog biscuits that come in five different flavors and colors. I like them, too, particularly the red ones. I know this because once, when Kady was three, we were fooling around and I told her I could eat a dog bone. She didn't believe me, so I bit off a hunk, chewed, and swallowed. Her eyes lit up, she grinned, then flipped out and started crying. So I did the only thing I could do: I licked the tears from Kady's face, nuzzled up against her and everything was fine.

*

WHILE I'M HERE I might as well look around, not that I think the ornament is really hiding with the mops, brooms, vacuum, and assorted rags that I have a strong suspicion are my missing shirts. Just looking at this stuff makes me think of all the chores I had to do when I was a kid.

In the house, my duties were limited. I was part of the storm window team — washing, installing, washing, and putting away for next year. Now and then I had to vacuum and dust. I still do that sometimes, but not unless I'm wearing the French Maid's costume, and that's only for special occasions.

I used to pity my sisters, though, because they were literally washerwomen, stuck in the basement helping my mom do the laundry for eleven people. Today they own an intergalactic chain of dry cleaners and it's payback time.

Mostly, I spent my chore years — sometimes called the "wonder years" because you always wonder why you're doing chores instead of playing with your friends — outside: mowing lawns in the summertime and raking leaves in the fall. Cutting the grass wasn't so bad, but raking leaves took almost all of Saturday. We had elms and maples with leaves as big as our faces and regularly filled sixty bags.

Residents of bordering communities could rake their leaves

right into the street and the city would come and scoop them up. But since we had to bag ours I think this easily explains my lifelong obsession with power lawn care equipment and labor-saving tools of all kinds. I didn't just make it up this stuff to get a laugh.

But I don't look back at my childhood chores with any sense of regret. Those were beautiful, timeless days full of smells and sensations that are hard for me to come by today.

My present household responsibilities are pretty basic: lawn care and vehicle maintenance. When I have time, I skim the pool, but that's rare. Depending on your point of view, I've either been robbed or relieved of most chores, and to tell you the truth, it's not such a good thing. Once, I used to love cleaning rain gutters. I'd get sweaty on a Saturday afternoon while Laura ran errands. Then I'd take a shower and at 5:30 we'd meet for a beer and a nice dinner. It was a great routine. Now my life is a more complicated. The house is bigger and it's not something that two people can handle by themselves.

So I fly my family in every other weekend to clean the place. I mean why not? They're used to it.

*

FAMILIES ARE FUNNY. They're living organisms bound by blood and emotion and the tightest knot of all — the knowledge of each other's secrets. If anyone wants out, they simply have to be killed.

Now you know why families try so damn hard to get along.

I come from a very large family. There're nine kids: David, Steven, me, Bruce, Billy, another David, Jeff, Kim, Becky, and Geoff. I'm third from the top. My mom had six of us with my dad. My stepdad, Bill, brought the other three along as part of the option package.

I think my mom and Bill were somehow destined to be together. They were old high school sweethearts but married other people. Then, Bill's wife was killed about the same time my dad died. When my mom and Bill discovered each was mate-less, they hooked up. And they're tremendously happy. Life is funny that way.

*

WHEN DEALING WITH my family — or anyone for that matter — I always try to practice the "Golden Rule." Stated plainly it is: "Treat others as you would like to be treated yourself." This is a lot better than "Fain el Kalb," which, in Arabic, literally means, "Where's the doggie?"

Following the spirit of the Golden Rule — which I think is essentially the process of loving — is a lot easier when you think of people not as "others," but as part of you.

With family, this comes with a bit less effort since there are little hints that you may be somehow related. For instance, you see your nose on the other person's face, and you both eat corn on the cob in a distressingly similar typewriter manner. And what else can explain the many times one or another of my brothers and I did the old "pull my finger" fart joke. Had an alien observed this ritual, there is no doubt we would have appeared as a single organism engaged in a natural act: pull finger, expel gas.

The Golden Rule is a lot harder to apply when extended to friends, community, and the human race. Sure, I know my brothers and sisters are part of me, but what about the Australian Bushman who just had a delicious breakfast of live termites, or the biker in Texas who's tickled pink over the purple tarantula he just had tattooed on his trachea. (I'd have chosen fuschia, but that's just me.) To do that I need to see some evidence of this connection or sameness in the natural world. So of course, I turn to my friends — the physics books.

As it turns out, many quantum physicists — the guys and gals who are supposed to know this stuff — also see the world as a seamless, unbroken wholeness; sort of how I like to think of my hot rod's front fenders. Fritjof Capra, in his book, *The Tao of Physics*, connects this physicists' view with the classic Oneness of Oriental mysticism, which *also* says that we are all interconnected. These days all physicists agree that on a subatomic level there are no hard edges and definitive borders. Everything is fuzzy and soft-edged, just like those big dice that people hang from their rear-view mirrors. It goes without saying that I wouldn't hang them in my car, but if I did, I wouldn't want to hear about it from anyone. And, in turn, I wouldn't criticize you. When you think about it, that attitude is a perfect reflection of the Golden Rule.

I know the question you're dying to ask: Can you prove we're all interconnected?

Well, yeah. According to the Big Bang theory the universe was once crammed into an unbelievably small "thing" called a singularity. An undivided Oneness if you will. Okay, think of it as every person on earth and all the animals, including the elephants, jammed into a very small elevator, only more so. I think you'll agree this suggests a certain intimacy. And a great big mess after the "bang."

After years of experimentation and playing with that magic eight ball that's always such a big hit at parties, physicists now know there's a limited or finite amount of matter in the universe. That means we're all made of . . . that's right . . . we're *all* made of the same recycled stuff. Carl Sagan calls it star stuff. In fact, scientists have estimated that every person on earth has some atoms in their body from every other person who ever existed. Yikes. This means I have atoms in my body from Buddha, Jesus, Lincoln, Geronimo, Hitler, Attila the Hun, Lassie, and Marilyn Monroe.

At least now I understand my mood swings.

We also continually swap atoms and molecules. Every time you exhale, tiny atomic pieces of your liver, kidneys, heart, and other internal organs get spewed into the room to be inhaled by everyone around — and vice versa. We are exchanging our internal organs. This is a level of intimacy that makes sexual contact seem like waving to somebody from a moving car.

Imagine that.

Now here's where the real magic comes in. In quantum physics there's something called Bell's Theorem which says reality is non-local. Bell is not referring to subway trains that run at rush hours and on weekends. What he means is that reality isn't what we see immediately surrounding us. Instead, the nature of reality is the interconnectedness of everything. Think about that.

Bell's Theorem was *proven* experimentally, which makes it as certain as bowling balls falling down, not up. Non-locality is a fact of life. Some might say it's *the* fact of life. But what's even more interesting about this is that Bell said that particles once joined — like everything in the universe today was once part of the initial singularity before the Big Bang — will forever influence each other instantaneously, and at any distance.

Let me put it in physics terms. Particles like electrons — for example — like to hang out in pairs, one having a left spin and one having a right spin. Think of it as a well balanced relationship: She likes ballet; he likes boxing. And it's okay with both of them. Even if later separated, when one particle's spin is reversed, its old partner will change its spin to compensate *at the same instant*. So now she boxes, he's in the tutu.

This may seem like no big deal if the electron couple just moved from the same house into adjoining condos. But what happens if one stays on Earth and the other goes to Alpha Centauri, four light years away? Same thing! Traveling at the speed of light, there's no time for one to send a message to the other saying, "Change your spin now." Yet it happens. Instantaneously. Wow.

That's non-locality.

What this means is that an Eskimo hunting seals in the arctic, a 400-pound Sumo wrestler in Japan changing his diaper, Cindy

Crawford changing *her* clothes, and you, and me, whether we realize it or not, all influence and are connected to each other.

Now, if I could only influence you, the Eskimo, and the wrestler to split and leave me and Cindy Crawford the hell alone, I'd be a happy guy.

While we're on the subject of the true nature of reality, I should tell you that in my studies I've discovered that the Golden Rule wasn't always Golden. Like all of life, it evolved from earlier attempts to quantify how people should treat each other.

Ancient scrolls found hidden in clay wine urns in a cave near the Dead Sea — in fact, in the cave right next door to where the Dead Sea scrolls were found — refer to something called the Mud Rule. Why mud and not gold? Well, you have to start somewhere. Besides, mud was quite valuable because of its many uses. Among them: building blocks for the great Egyptian cities, writing tablets, and a life-extending elixir popularized by the boy Pharaoh, Tutankhamen.

The Mud Rule's text has been roughly translated as, "This is my mud, get your own mud!" Not very neighborly, but when you think about those testy biblical Egyptians, not unexpected.

Subsequent versions of the Rule, as documented in the secret archives of the Vatican Museum, are the Iron Rule, the Napoleonic Rule, the Slide Rule, the Infield Fly Rule, the rule of the road, the rule of thumb, and the still indecipherable Rula Lenska.

*

I MAY BE PART of an unbroken wholeness on a very deep, primal level, yet I don't want to have to sacrifice my uniqueness. But do I have to? I think I see the way clear: The trouble starts when we define uniqueness as separateness. That's when the Golden Rule gets forgotten. That's when everything bad, from pollution to murder to the Neilsen ratings, starts happening. Do you know why

I don't get up one morning and decide to put Big Jim and the Twins in the toaster oven just for the heck of it? Obviously, it would cause me enormous pain because they're a part of me. A favorite part. Think of each other, and the planet, the same way.

Even though the physicists have proved it and the Eastern mystics have always believed it, I also know intuitively that we're all part of one another. This is why I look forward to the day when the Prime Minister of Israel signs a peace treaty with the Palestinian leader and then turns and says to him, "Now, pull my finger."

The spirit of God — or if you like, the true nature of the universe — is in all people and things. But it's kind of hard for me at the moment to think in terms of a concept that incredibly large and complex. So I see it like a glass of beer. The white, foamy head seems separate from the amber liquid supporting it, but . . . the head is the world of matter and energy, basically the universe as we know it. The tiny bubbles in the foam are us, as unique individuals. The layer of amber liquid is God. But in reality, it's all beer!

*

I JUST SWITCHED ON the Christmas videotape, and tears are streaming down my face. I can't get over the memory of how tasty mom's turkey was, and of all the good cheer, and the joy of gift opening on Christmas morn — all of which I'm experiencing again on the screen in front of me. It's also possible that I'm crying because I'm remembering the smoke that filled the house when I started that fire with the chimney flue closed. It was so bad we nearly had to have Christmas dinner on the front lawn. I wanted to open the flue, but do you know how hard it is to find the damn flue handle without ruining the sleeve of your nifty new Christmas outfit? Here's something else for the philosophers to tackle: Why do you always get cool toys when you believe in Santa, and clothes ever after?

Anyway, when my family gets together in one place, the logistics are daunting. The last time was for my brother David's wedding, though to tell you the truth, I'm still not sure *which* brother David got married.

When we all meet, things can get bit weird. I believe that's because we're all saying the same thing to ourselves: "My, *they're* getting older."

When we're all together I sometimes get the feeling that they might think that it's difficult having me as a brother. One reason is because not everyone in the family is . . . er, well, as financially fluid as I am. I know it's best to avoid using the childhood phrase, "I make more money than you do, nanner, nanner, nanner." The only family member who comes close to the kind of power and influence I wield is young Dave. He works at Los Alamos, where he is busy developing the home version of the atomic bomb.

Still, I try not to be insensitive about my good fortune and thoughtlessly rub it in their faces. Actually — and please don't tell them — but at times, I completely envy their lifestyles. But a brother has a responsibility to dish it out! I also understand that even though they have great lives and great families, it's hard to live in the long shadow of the many fantastic things they think I've accomplished. Because of the road I've traveled — from being a guest of the State to being a guest in millions of living rooms — I recognize that when I come to our get-togethers, I bring lots of baggage. That's why I'm a very generous tipper when my family helps me carry it all into the house. Besides, it's *their* presents.

At Christmas-time, when we're sitting around in front of a fireplace filled with crackling Yule logs, I find that it's the older folks — parents, grandparents, aunts, uncles — and the tourists we insist stay behind the velvet ropes and on the rubber runners, who are usually the most interested in my work. They all want to know about the TV and movie business. They want to hear stories about the celebrities I've met. They never stop asking me what Jonathan

Taylor Thomas is really like, and frankly, I'm tired of this because I'm the one responsible for his entire career.

Of course, my family is not unwilling to use me now and then, when it comes to their friends. It all starts with the sentence, "Have you seen *Home Improvement*?"

And then there's Kady who likes to smile and say, "My dad's Santa Claus." Good thing she's more of a clothes person than a toy person.

Sometimes being Santa Claus can help compensate for being the center of attention. One year I put solid gold picture frames from Tiffany under the tree for everyone, with a wonderful portrait of me as Santa already included. Another time, I bought computers and modems so we could go online, stay in touch by E-mail, and keep up with each other at any moment. It's really brought us closer together. But not everyone is as into the computer as I am. A couple of my brothers don't write very often. One just sends pictures of naked women that he picks up on the Internet. I don't look at them, of course. That's my story and I'm stickin' to it.

The truth is that we all get along wonderfully. We've seen each other through the highs and lows. My family is pretty much immune to the yin and yang, the good and bad, and the adult and child in me. They accept those. What they truly like about me is the Comic. I've always made them laugh. That's the constant. The Comic has made bad situations better. The Comic has been generous. The Comic is a nice guy who always gives the family a discount at the door and covers the two-drink minimum.

*

T HE COMIC ALSO HAS another family: a TV family.
Although we deal with real issues, the Taylors are not exactly real, even though according to quantum physicists it's hard to say what's real and what's not these days. I go by the orange juice

test. If at least 20 percent comes from real oranges, it satisfies the legal requirements, and I'm pretty sure Anita Bryant concurs.

The Taylors live by a sitcom formula. Any problem that exists needs to be solved in about 23 minutes. Real family problems can stay unresolved for a lifetime. Or put it this way: If this were an episode of *Home Improvement*, Tim Taylor would have found the hood ornament by now, blown it up, Jill would have proven him silly, and Wilson would have adequately explained his behavior through some old Tibetan tribal ritual. Tim Taylor not only survives, but hopefully grows wiser through the experience, and our 23 minutes are up.

My TV family is very important to me because during the shooting year I probably spend more time with them than I do with my real family. It's a good experience for all of us, and a creative way to circumvent the polygamy laws. Pat Richardson (who plays my wife, Jill) and I protect the boys who play our sons. We parent on the set. Actually, it's more like grandparent. We get the best of the kids, but don't have to feed them or pay for their college education. Occasionally I slip into the role of a weird uncle. I do "fart" and "fake vomit" jokes all day long. In other words, I'm a great influence on those kids because they learn by my behavior what they *shouldn't* be doing.

My relationship with Pat is pretty much like something she once said. "It's just like a good marriage: We're best friends and we have no sex."

Sometimes we all wish we were the Taylors. Does this sound weird? The sitcom rules notwithstanding, they function on a very high level most of the time. They discuss and get over problems. (You can do this, too. It's the communication, not the speed of resolution, that's important.) There's a lot of love. Both parents are involved, and are happy with themselves and in their relationship. That happiness shows. So I looked into hiring the brilliant writers on my show to script and resolve my *real* life, but their salaries are too high.

I'm not saying there isn't room on TV for single parents, divorced couples, two-father or two-mother households, kids with magic powers, childless couples, people too dysfunctional to find love, couples with alien children, or aliens themselves, but that's not all there is. The Taylors just want to live satisfying lives as a family, have fun, and not burn down the house. Our "edge" — if you can call it that — is our normality.

Tim Taylor is exactly the same age as I am. Unlike me, his life is pretty calm. He married his college sweetheart. He has a dream job. He has a sidekick with a thick skin. He loves what he does. He's not that much different than me, after all.

There are times I've definitely wanted to be just like Tim Taylor. God, yes. He has everything I want in life without any of the baggage. (Being a well-meaning menace to society isn't a negative, is it?) He has three boys, lives in Detroit, and is a local celebrity. He gets to fool with tools and cars all day long. He gets to be on TV, be a smartass, and go home to a loving family. He was created out of my fantasies of a simple and idyllic life.

Unlike me, Tim Taylor isn't burdened with thoughts about the cosmos. He thinks the Cosmos are a soccer team. He hasn't had a full-blown midlife crisis yet. The only thing he's blown is a camshaft. His life has unfolded too nicely for him to be worried about the nature of subatomic particles. Sand particles in his bathing suit after a day at the lake are troublesome enough. If I was to talk with him over some beers about what's going on with me, I know exactly what he'd say:

"Whoa. So let me get this straight. You think that the head on this beer is the world of matter and energy? Or are you saying you think something's the matter because you have no energy?"

"The first one. Just what if? And the tiny bubbles in the foam are us as unique individuals . . . "

"And the beer itself is . . . ?"

"Well, you know, like God. All people and all things."

"Check, please. Jill was right about you; if you promise me you won't talk to my kids about this I'll give you a ride home. I've got Pink Floyd's *Dark Side of the Moon!*"

Tim Taylor will never get the bigger picture. Wilson, maybe. Al would enjoy the conversation, but Tim? Forget it.

Tim Taylor is my vocation. I play this guy on TV. I'm always playing. I started as Tim Dick. Then I played Tim Allen on the comedy stage; now I play Tim Allen playing Tim Taylor.

I guess what this all boils down to is that the Toolman is actually my second cousin, once removed.

*

SPEAKING OF PLAYING, I'll head into the den. This is where the family gathers and dammit, I miss my family, even though they've only been gone a few hours. The TV is this room's centerpiece. It's an ominous black structure that reminds me of the obelisk in *2001: A Space Odyssey*. It's such a major part of our lives that it's almost a fourth family member.

This TV is always on. I don't know why, but it just seems to be the way TV has evolved. Remember when TV went off the air at 11:00 p.m.? We heard the *Star-Spangled Banner*, saw some jets and the American flag, then the test pattern and the beeeeeeeeeep that ran from sign-off until sign-on the next morning, for the farm report. Today, the only time I hear that beeping sound is at an industry movie screening when everyone's pagers go off at once.

The next place to look for the hood ornament is the den closet.

Nope, not in here. How do I know when I've done nothing more than look inside? Easy, it's so packed that there's not enough room to hold the trimmings from my last haircut. It's stuffed full of my boxes. The top shelf is crammed with hats. The clothes rack is jammed with about 30 varsity letterman-style jackets, the kind with big graphics on the back that companies give away as promotional items. Laura hates them.

"Keep the *Home Improvement* 100th Show jacket with the cool leather sleeves, but dump the rest," she always says.

"Why? They may come in handy."

"When? There's only six days of winter in Los Angeles. Besides, all you need to do is wear a jacket with the *Toy Story* or *The Santa Clause* logo on it and it will be like walking out of the house with a balloon animal stuck on your head. It's not as if people can't already pick you out of a crowd."

I suppose she's right, at least about being spotted in public. But if Laura knew physics like I, who have read a couple books on the subject, know physics, she'd know that the best way to get rid of stuff is to just leave it in one place long enough and it will disappear on its own.

Anyone who wears socks is familiar with this phenomenon. While it's tough for any one object to retain its form, when a pair of something is involved, the odds against both having the same life-span are tremendous. Invariably, one sock simply vanishes and you can never find it again, no matter how often you retrace your steps from the hamper, to the washer, to the drier. You can pick through the used fabric softener sheets and drier lint all you want — ain't gonna find it.

According to hosiery experts, white athletic socks are the most common victims. However, sportswear scientists can't agree about the cause, what *really* happens, or where the socks go. Some think the sweat-absorption rate is a key factor. Others cite the elastic band half-life. A small group of researchers categorically rejects both ideas, and insists that according to the laws of the conservation of matter and energy, that for a sock to actually lose molecular cohesion and vanish it would have to change from matter into energy — and that the transformation would require the sock to travel at the speed of light multiplied by itself, or 186,000 miles per second squared.

More likely, they say, the socks are just hiding and having a good time at our expense. Then, when we throw away the single, they pair up again and move to Borneo, where no one wears socks, and the natives kill and eat anyone who does. Bear in mind that this Sock Sanctuary explanation is still just a theory.

The closest I've come to learning the secret was once, years ago, when I was about to put on my sneakers and socks for a little pickup basketball. Just as I reached for the drawer handle, I thought I heard voices from within.

"I have to go. You'll find someone else."

"I won't. I can't. Not after being with you."

"Don't be ridiculous."

"I'll suffer."

"Promise you won't try to stop me."

"What can I do? It's your life. But you'll be back — and I might not be waiting."

I opened the drawer and found no socks at all. Then I realized I'd been listening to the couple next door.

Will we ever know the truth about socks?

Like most other secrets of the universe, probably not.

*

OUR EARTHQUAKE KIT is on the closet floor. For a moment, this startles me, since I thought the kit was in my office. But I remember that Laura wanted one for both places and both of our cars. I think she also buried one in a time capsule in the back yard in case sometime in the future we had an earthquake and ran out of supplies. That's planning ahead. Way ahead.

Now that I think about it, it was just after the Northridge earthquake that I began losing things. The art portfolio, the Christmas tape, and the hood ornament. Maybe things are missing around here because my house was nearly destroyed. It seems like a reasonable explanation. Between the shaking, packing, unpacking, packing again, and finally unpacking, either a lot of our stuff got misplaced, or escaped to Borneo, where socks roam free.

I'M HUNGRY. There's lots of stuff to eat in the kitchen pantry so all I have to do is decide. What about this cereal box with the big red letters that read, "Free Inside!" The box looks new but, wait, the bent top can only mean one thing: Kids. If I know my daughter, she's already fished around inside for the prize. No, I recognize this box. The prize was lousy.

What is it about surprises? Everybody loves them as long as the "IRS" doesn't appear anywhere on the package. When I was young, my brothers and I would have opened cereal boxes and stolen the prizes right in the supermarket, if our parents wouldn't have had us arrested for trying. As it is, I had so many brothers that by the time I got to the box at home, whatever was inside was gone — including the cereal.

These days it's hardly worth it. Most cereals don't have surprises and those that do only have cheesy stuff. Instead of a toy that inspires your childhood fantasies, now you get some flat piece of thick paper that you unfold. Inside is a picture of a duck. Move the tab and his ears wiggle. Big deal.

Now kids' prizes have moved from the cereal boxes to the frozen dinners and most significantly to the fast food restaurant. It's grown quite sophisticated. Now, McDonald's, Burger King, and the rest give away toys that, to be perfectly honest, are clearly worth far more than any meal they accompany. Pretty soon the competition will get so out of hand that no kid will come in unless they get a $300 bicycle with each thirty-cent hamburger.

"I'll have the Happy Meal and the Schwinn, please."

There will have be something for the adults, too.

"I'll have the Combo Deluxe. That comes with the Harley, right?"

"Yes sir. That will be $4.28. Please show your current driver's license and proof of insurance at window two, and pick up your promotional items at the warehouse across the street."

Laura left a chicken breast for me in the refrigerator, but it's too much trouble. I'd have to heat it. What else do I see: green olives, American cheese, strawberries, refried beans, noodles left over from three nights ago. Laura can do anything with leftovers. Like a sculptor who sees the finished statue within the block of granite and chips away the stone to set it free, Laura sees unlimited possibilities in a Tupperware bowl of mashed potatoes. Me? If the food isn't sitting there, on the plate, already made, I don't see any possibilities, except possibly going out.

Here's my excuse: I rarely even make my own lunch. On the *Home Improvement* set, someone brings it to me. On a movie set, someone brings it to me. This is what the restaurant lifestyle is all about. I'm not lazy. If I were, I'd have my food pre-chewed. Also, it's not really cost-effective in my home to stock things I like unless it's in a can. For instance, fresh turkey is out because the longest I've ever known turkey to last is four months, if you don't mind the bluish edge. That's why we have lots of canned chili, canned beans, canned hash, canned Spam. I think you know where we're going here: I've got major intestinal problems.

Any minute now I'll make up my mind. Let me check the pantry again. Hmm. I didn't see this Lipton's chicken noodle soup before. I like this stuff. You add the packet contents to boiling water and stir. What you get is some sort of noodle in yellow salt water. I like salt. This is good. What else? I know, a turkey bologna sandwich with potato chips.

I know I said earlier I wouldn't consider turkey bologna. I changed my mind. Think of it as my concession to today's new health consciousness, which is a lot like the old health consciousness, only much more expensive. Anyway, I'd rather be safe than sorry. I suddenly remembered that I'd heard *real* bologna is now poisonous. In fact, supposedly everything I ate as a child is now on the FDA's restricted list. (They can't restrict you from eating it, but you are restricted from later saying they didn't warn you.) Bologna didn't seem poisonous when I was young, but according to recent studies it apparently stays in your system and kills you slowly, like an arsenic IV.

I'll be making my sandwich with Wonder Bread. There's something about Wonder Bread. It's comfort food. It sticks to everything — your teeth, your gums, your ribs, and your shoe. Two pieces wrapped around a hunk of turkey bologna, a slice of American cheese, a bit of mayo, and a dash of mustard, and I feel like I'll live forever.

I can see the soup is almost finished cooking and I'm proud to say I cooked it myself. I'm what you call a low-maintenance guy. I can measure water, pour it into a pot, bring it to a rapid boil, and let it simmer. I'm very good with a simmer. Laura just turns off the flame, but I believe that when the instructions say to simmer, I simmer. I'm sure the Lipton people thought carefully about how to get the most instructions onto the least amount of package space, so if they didn't want us to simmer they wouldn't have used the word. It's not up for debate.

Laura and I disagree a lot about directions. She doesn't read the instructions on powdered soup mixes; she thinks she knows how to do it. But there's a science to this. The people at Lipton Labs don't screw around. They want to do it right. I've even heard that they sometimes invite Mrs. Paul and Betty Crocker to consult.

If Betty Crocker says it, I do it. When I read "Preheat oven to 350," I wait for that light to go off. I don't pop it in there early and have to adjust later. I always put it on a greased cookie sheet. I listen to *exactly* what she says. That's why I can bake a Betty Crocker cake and why my wife fails miserably. She always misses. Either it's a little doughy in the middle or burnt on the outside. But Betty has learned this. There are rules. You go by those rules.

Now that lunch is ready, I'll sit in the den, kick back, flip on the TV, and maybe even read a little physics. What would you call this tableau if Norman Rockwell painted it? *Middle-aged Guy Who Should Know Better?*

*

SOMETIMES I'D LIKE to walk out the front door, turn left, and get completely lost.

We all have our escape fantasies — especially those of us who think we're caught forever. I read once that Sally Field said her favorite cartoon panel was of a woman, trapped behind and desperately gripping some prison bars. The thing is that she was actually holding a *little section* of bars in front of her face. She could have put them down and walked away anytime.

I didn't take off when Kady was born, and I don't believe I could or would take off now, but I think about it. Sometimes I think, "Enough with the responsibility to family, friends, employees. It's a big world. There are other lives I could lead. I could just disappear."

I think I once saw this story on *Outer Limits*.

I'd like to visit other worlds: other planets, dimensions, parallel universes, inner space. I'd need a ship that's somewhat baroque in design, sort of Jules Verne meets *Forbidden Planet*. Very comfortable. Plush seats. Under the hood would be a propulsion system capable of taking me everywhere, and at the same time not be too much machine to run to the corner for a quart of milk. Just think how much fun it would be to meet aliens, check how other possible lives turned out, or pop up in some physicist's quantum experiment and have a new particles — you know, a *taon* — named after me.

Kady and Laura would, of course, come along. (Wouldn't want to escape!) Everything would be a new adventure. Frankly, I could use one right now. I need to get some fresh air. Anyway, I have to run some errands for Laura, and I promised to stop by the speed shop I partly own. Maybe I left the ornament there by mistake. Who knows? Stranger things have happened.

Recently.

SIX

I'VE GOT TO GET OUT of the house. I've got to run some errands. I should buy something for dinner. I may love bologna and potato chips, but I didn't make it to mid-life by ignoring my four basic food groups. Or did I?

It looks like a nice day. I could even take a drive. I just need to find my wallet and car keys. Now where did I put them? There — on the kitchen counter. Things are looking up already.

Everything's great except for this: I'm afraid to get into the car. Is that an unreasonable fear? I don't think so. Don't forget when I drove it this morning, I nearly mowed down some innocent pedestrians. Human beings that mean something to other human beings. I was literally inches away from changing their lives forever. My life forever. It's absolutely frightening. I'm not kidding around.

But it didn't happen, so things go on as usual. I'll pull myself together.

*

I T'S AMAZING HOW LIFE *can* change in an instant. For me, it happened more than once: when my dad died, when I went to prison, when I got famous. Actually, the part about becoming well-known didn't happen *that* quickly, but I understand that from where the reader might be it probably looks like an overnight thing. One minute I'm saying "men are pigs" to a trailer park crowd at the Chuckle Hut in Pismo Beach, and the next I'm proving it in a top ten sitcom and some hit movies. The truth is that it takes years of hard work, an uncle in the business, or your kid attending the same kindergarten as Steven Spielberg's kid, to create the kind of success that people notice.

The reason celebrity seems so instantaneous is because unless you're paying strict attention and following the tedium of some-one's career, when a performer "makes it" because of a big movie/TV show/album/book, the sensory impact of their voice and image suddenly appearing everywhere in the media is a lot like an atomic bomb exploding. There's the mushroom cloud. Look too closely and you'll go blind. Stand around and the shock wave will blow you over.

The truth is that you devote years to creating the right condi-tions and the correct mixture of elements to reach the critical mass necessary for detonation. You're alone, down in your laboratory, trying over and over. If and when you get it right, if luck smiles on you a bit, if you've remembered to wear your radiation suit so that you don't get fatally burned too early in the experiment, only then does your life become deadly calm for one second, and smash into the mass consciousness the next — like Fat Man or Little Boy hurtling toward an unsuspecting Japanese city.

However, compared to making the media and the public sit up and take notice of *anything*, exploding nuclear bombs seems simple.

Celebrity is unstable. It can live for a Millivanillisecond

(followed by a big sucking sound), or endure for 2000 Christian years. Why? Who knows? The proper conditions are elusive, even whimsical, and are always subject to change. I think it's luck, and talent helps. Oh, and stick-to-it-iveness. If this was so easy to figure out, everyone would be famous and not have to wait in line for their fifteen minutes. (And I'm talking about positive stuff, not being the moron who murdered John Lennon.) And incidentally, I do believe in Andy Warhol's "everyone's famous for fifteen minutes" theory. It's just that for some, their fifteen minutes are a hell of a lot longer than for others.

What's interesting is that when most everybody finally knows who you are, that's when *you* finally learn something extremely important: the true meaning of the word "anonymity." I think the old cliché put it best: "You don't miss the water if the milk's for free." No, it's "Don't buy the cow until the well runs dry." Wait. It's that you don't miss anything until it's gone. Someone wrote a song about this once. I can't remember who sang it, but you know what I'm talking about.

Not that I'm complaining. Without the attention I'd just be a very talented actor/comedian toiling anonymously down in my laboratory. So, uh . . . most of the time the attention is okay. I like it. No, I love it. But occasionally I'd like to be invisible again. That way, when I go to Disneyland or McDonald's, it would be "Tim Dick and his family," not Tim Allen and those faceless people who just happen to be tagging along. Every once in a while I'd just like to be my unselfconscious self.

You most likely take your anonymity for granted, but *you* can comfortably retrieve an annoying booger, or reach down for a quick groin area adjustment in public without the worry that some photographer might capture it for a two-page spread in *The Globe* the following week: *Tim Allen's Struggle . . . with a Booger!*

I wish I had a bit of that back, but that's a pretty tall order. Yet, sometimes it happens. I once met a guy at a cocktail party. We talked for a few moments and he finally said, "I'm sorry for being rude: What do you do?" A Disney executive sitting next to me tried to cover my feelings, thinking I'd take offense. "C'mon, Dan," he said to the guy, "this is Tim Allen . . . *Home Improvement*? . . . *The Santa Clause*? . . . *Toy Story*? Buzz Lightyear?"

"Sorry, I don't watch movies or TV," Dan said. He had no clue who I was, and it was great because he liked me for me.

A similar thing happened at my 20-year high school reunion. Near the end of the evening, after I was presented with a big hammer and people talked about *Home Improvement* and made jokes about *Tool Time*, a guy I'd known in school came up and said, "Jesus, must be 20 years!"

I said, "Yeah, it has, Brian. That's why we're at the 20-year reunion."

"So what have you been doing, man?" he said, staring at me. Waiting. I realized he honestly had no clue. I also realized he must have been in the hotel bar during the whole event. So I told him a little about my TV show, but all he said was, "I think maybe someone told me about that. But I'm not sure."

His naiveté was so refreshing that I slipped something in his drink and when he died I had him stuffed for display in my living room. As a pleasant reminder.

Both occurrences were, unfortunately, exceptions to the rule. The only place I have real anonymity is at my house. Once, after not seeing Laura all day, we met, quite by accident, in the living room. She said, "Who are you and how did you get in?"

*

FIRST STOP: the speed shop. It's a balmy afternoon. The traffic is light, which only happens when Laura is not in the car. I'm nearly to the speed shop. I had a thought: Maybe they have something around the garage that I can use on the hot rod hood instead of the ornament. Of course, for all I know I might have left the damn thing there in the first place.

The speed shop is in the end unit of an industrial tract building. My friend Ron runs it. It's a great place to watch men working with their hands. There's a little balcony I like to watch the shop from. It kind of gives me that "Lee Iacocca admiring his factory" feeling. Hot rodders are good people.

Because I'm a part owner, I get to keep a few of my cars in the garage. I store the hot rod from the TV show, another car that I want to redo, and an English rally car. I bought the rally car a long time ago, but I can't drive it because it's not certified.

Ron is working on a car when I pull up.

Before I can get down to business, Ron wants to show me six different projects his guys are building. He's most proud of a restored 1969 Camaro.

"The customer decided he wanted the fastest Camaro on the planet."

"Why?"

"Just because."

"All right!"

Typical guy behavior. But he came to the right place. Ron and his crew do great things.

What you may not know is that I belong to a neat species called "men." With our spare income and in our spare time, we will build absolutely stupid things. And the beauty is that other guys actually admire this and the men who do it. It's good to see men dedicate themselves to craft instead of violence. It's not just work. It's a Zen experience. A oneness with process. We learn about patience. There's a relationship between men and their machines that goes way beyond what we can put into words. (Ironically, there's a relationship between women and words that goes way beyond what men could ever comprehend.) Besides, who can hear anyone talking above the roar of the engines?

Finally, Ron lets me get in a few words of my own. But when I explain my problem he's not much help.

"Remember the hood ornament I got for my Ford hot rod? I can't find it anywhere. I thought maybe I left it here."

"Haven't seen it. What was it like again?"

I describe it, but Ron just scratches his head.

"No company ever made anything like that."

"Well, I *do* have it," I say. Oh, oh. Being defensive.

"The guy told you it was from an old Packard?" Ron takes his car books off the shelf and leafs through. "These are all the hood ornaments," he says, pointing to pages of pictures. "They never made one like that. I don't think *any* manufacturer did. He might have been bullshitting you."

"I can't believe that."

"The only thing I can think of is a car made in Venezuela a long time . . . "

"Why'd you say that?"

"Say what?"

"Venezuela?"

"No reason."

"You said there was a car made in Venezuela."

"No, I didn't."

"Yes, you did."

"Okay, I did. What's the big deal?"

"Why would you say Venezuela? Why would you even *say* that?"

"What's with you, Tim?"

"Of all places, why did you pick Venezuela? Have you ever been there?"

"No. I don't know. They just had a coup there, and the supreme military commander loved cars and had a one-off sedan manufactured. As soon as the car was delivered . . . "

"What?"

"It was just a joke."

"What was the joke?"

"The part about the car ever being delivered."

"Any other word you could have come up with besides Venezuela?"

"You got a problem with Venezuela?"

"No. It's just that . . . "

We both stop as a group of kids run by the open door, chasing a ball, having a great time. They remind me of how I used to go with my dad to his shop.

"That kid's shirt is the color of the Venezuelan flag," says Ron.

"Stop that!"

Ron can barely contain his laughter. I'd probably laugh too, if he wasn't being so bizarre. I know for a fact that Ron has never been to Venezuela. But I don't think I'll get anywhere if I pursue the point. Better to let it drop.

"The hot rod has to be ready Monday morning," I say. "If I can't find the ornament, I can't give them the car. The thing is special to me. I bought it first and built the car afterwards. They belong together."

"Maybe I can find something around here for you to use just in case," Ron suggests. "I can drop it by tonight."

Ron is a great guy and an artist under the hood, not to mention someone with a strange sense of humor. He's an honest mechanic who, unlike so many people I know, has no agenda. It's nice. Because of who I am, I can make a big difference in some people's lives. I will if it's the right thing to do, but there are some people who find it hard to be around me because of that. They want something from me. I can feel it. Sometimes they'll come out and ask. More often they won't. I'm not saying this is bad — everyone wants things; me, too — but the unspoken desires can often get in the way of any intimacy. I may be overly sensitive, or imagining things, but I keep waiting for the other shoe to drop and the truth to come out that they really want something. I'd rather it be out in the open. Just don't ask me to bear your children.

Ron wants nothing from me, however he's clearly appreciative of the opportunity. He gives to charity, takes care of his family. He's a generous and grounded man, and that's why when I need help he understands.

"Where'd you find this hood ornament, anyway?" he asks. "Venezuela?"

"Will you cut that out? Have you been talking to my wife?"

Ron has to get back to work, and I have other stuff to do. Besides, I suddenly feel very tired. I check my watch. As I expected, it's four p.m. This time every day my low blood sugar thing kicks in.

All right, I'll stop by the market and pick up some dinner. A man's meal: a good strip steak, rub a little Roquefort cheese on it, grill it. Have some cut beans and a salad with blue cheese dressing.

*

DRIVING HOME from the studio each night, I pass this market. But I've never gone in. When I shop, I go to stores in my neighborhood. It's not only because they're convenient, but because the people there know me. The checkout lady always has a sunny smile for me when I come in, and I don't think it's because I'm famous. When she finally quits asking to sign my name in marker on different parts of her body, I'll be sure. Also, I don't have to worry about what I buy. For example, in a strange drug store I have to pretty much stick to buying aspirin or the clerks will whisper, "Oh boy, the Toolman's got a little hemorrhoid problem."

The minute I walk through the automatic doors into this hangar-like food emporium I realize I've once again mistakenly assumed I'm a normal guy who can go into any store at any time. This market is strange and dangerous territory and I'm quickly immobilized. My immediate problem: I have absolutely no idea where the meat counter is.

Also, now that I'm inside, the ten minute warning begins ticking in my head. This means I have about that much time before people notice me and shopping becomes impossible. Think of this as the shopper's version of football's two-minute drill. I'll have to move quickly.

Luckily, I've found the meat department. First, I had to get through the dog food and shoe polish department and the canned beans and tampons departments. I've never figured out the reasons behind why one product is put next to another. If you have a clue, please write in.

Anyway, the steaks don't look so good, in fact they look like the meat that started the mutiny on the *Bounty*, and the butcher is on a break. There's already a little line milling around between the pork chops and the pesto sausage and they look vaguely similar to the faces I saw in the produce isle — mustn't dawdle. The Curious are blatantly staring at me. They must somehow see though my disguise.

Oh, I didn't tell you?

Sometimes when I go out in public I wear my glasses to confuse people who *think* I'm me, but can't be completely sure. I can fool some of the people, some of the time . . . Okay, It mostly doesn't work, but it has on occasion given me the extra second or two I need to make a hasty escape. I have great empathy for Superman. How would you feel if your greatest triumph was fooling Lois Lane, the most monumentally stupid woman on the planet? She can't recognize him because of the glasses? Perhaps she needs the glasses.

I should move on before I start a commotion. I've had many memorable fan encounters, and know what can happen. Most, of course, are pleasant, but sometimes the wackos come out of the woodwork and it feels like I'm starring in an episode of "The Fugitive."

For instance, airports can be a dangerous place. Once a guy saw me and Kady getting some frozen yogurt. He grabbed his wife, and whispered, "That's Tim Allen!!"

She stared for a second and shook her head. "I don't think so. No."

Talk about blind. They were only four feet away. Just to prove he was right, the man yelled to my profile, "Hey, Tim!"

It took all my acting ability, which is minor, not to flinch, move an eyebrow, or let my pupils dilate.

"Tim! Tool Man!"

Nothing.

"I told you it wasn't him, you idiot," hissed his wife, now completely embarrassed. "Imagine yelling at some poor guy. What if he looked up?"

"But honey, I could swear . . . "

As they headed toward their gate I could still hear the wife's badgering as their voices trailed off, and I gotta tell you I kind of felt for the guy. I keep getting this image of her telling the story at cocktail parties. "Go ahead Bob, tell everyone how you stuck your big foot in your mouth when you thought you saw Tim Allen."

Bob's busy downing his fifth scotch.

Geez. Bob, if you're reading this book — it was me. Sorry.

Sometimes it's the *Twilight Zone*. On the way home from my in-laws one Christmas day, I pulled into a rest stop with a brand new McDonald's and a filling station on the highway between Detroit and Flint, Michigan. Seemed like a great idea: You could get gas in either place. Inside there were two people sweeping the floor and a young woman behind the counter. My family was asleep in the car.

"Can I have a cup of tea, please?" I said.

I could see the hot water right behind the counter. She looked at me, stared for a couple seconds, and said "I'll have to go in the back and check." When she returned she had the assistant manager in tow.

"Can I have some tea?" I asked him.

"Let me go see if we have any," he said, with a blank expression. He went into the back and two different guys came out.

"Can I have a cup of tea, now, please?" I asked.

"Gotta check in the back," they said together, like a couple Stepford Wives.

Then the girl and the assistant manager and the two workers reappeared and they all stared as though I was Madonna, naked. Then one of the guys said, "I think we've got some tea in the back." He disappeared and came back with the manager, who said, "We understand you want some tea."

"Yes."

"Give him some tea!" he barked. "We have the tea right here."

I can appreciate what happened. These fine people didn't want to alarm me. They thought if they moved very slowly I wouldn't leave. It's the ol' "deer in the woods" approach. I can even imagine them meeting in the back, right after I placed my order, to plan their strategy.

GIRL: "That's Tim Allen out front. He wants tea."

ASSISTANT MANAGER: "Let's use some psychology on him."

TWO GUYS: "Yeah. If we all move real slow we can hold off on the tea and get a chance to look at him longer. We don't want to scare him."

GIRL: "Do we serve tea?"

Little did they know that had they produced a salt lick, I may have eaten right out of their hands.

*

WHAT DO FOLKS WANT? Usually an autograph or a few moments of my time to chat. They want that personal connection, and a story to tell their friends. Most of the time I am pleased to oblige, and happy to have done something that's emotionally touched another person. However, I draw the line at giving away undergarments or body parts. But I gladly accept them.

I certainly don't mind doing this stuff, no matter how much I've carped about the loss of anonymity. After all, by tuning into my show, people invite me into their homes. Or they come to my movies. This is what I always wanted.

The problem is, it's also, at times, what I don't want. So what I *do* is stand back and watch it all happen from a mental distance. I see people stare at me with the same kind of look you give someone who's got a handicap. Look, look away, then look again. Then my favorite: feign an activity to create a closer proximity.

I'm guilty of it myself.

When I met Clint Eastwood, I shook like a proton in a super-collider. He's powerful. No one fools with Clint. Any Joe Blow off the street will come up to me and sit in my lap. I'm accessible. They know me from TV as the fallible, fun guy from next door. Now *that's* approachable. But Eastwood? I think he's got a handgun in his pants. This guy has shot so many people — even if it's only in the movies — you have reason to be afraid.

We met a few years ago when I was performing at a comedy club in L.A. I told the owner someone might be looking for me.

"Clint Eastwood?" he said. "Sure Tim, Clint Eastwood." My manager jumped in to add, "Eastwood never goes out."

As if on cue, Clint appeared at the door going, "I'm looking for Tim Allen." The entire place went, *"He's looking for Tim Allen!"* It was perfect because it was really loud, with that cool delivery. *"Eastwood's here to see Allen."*

Clint walked in and empty chairs pushed themselves out of the way as he moved past. It was the strangest thing. Then he sat down with us. I said, "Do you want something to drink? What do you drink?"

He narrowed his eyes and in his famous whisper said, "I'll have what you're having."

My brand! Believe me, nothing I've ever done since has made me feel like more of a man. I wanted to stand on top of the table and shout, "Hey, did you hear that! Clint wants what I'm having!" That feeling translated physically into my best, contained subtle nod (about 8 degrees down and back), coupled with a slight wry smile, only out of one corner of my mouth. That's the cool way. Oh, who am I trying to kid. I was grinning ear to ear like a goofy ten-year-old boy.

I was just as nervous when I met Arnold Schwarzenegger. I saw him at an Academy Awards party. Finally I walked up and introduced myself. And wouldn't you know it, he's *exactly* like I expected. He gave me the once over and said, "You should verk out more, yer love handles are showing."

He made me feel so comfortable that pretty soon I took my life into my hands and imitated him to his face.

I said, "Vat did you zink about zis?"

He said, "Iz zat how I zound to you, huh? Hahaha!"

Our wives ignored it all and talked about day care centers and dumb husbands instead.

Then Arnold said, "I hope zat yule stop by for a cigar and some schnapps some day. Not zis schnapps ve drink here." He slapped me hard on the chest and I hand-signaled Laura to call 9-1-1. "*Real* schnapps. Schnapps that puts you on your *ass*."

I was so flustered from meeting Arnold that when Jane Fonda and Ted Turner came over and joined the conversation, I turned to Jane and said, "I love your dad. I'm a big, big fan. How is he?"

The silence could have stopped a Peterbuilt. I forced a half-smile and waited.

She wasn't smiling.

Then I realized her dad was dead. Now *my* wife tells *this one* at our cocktail parties. "Go ahead Tim, tell everyone how you stuck your big foot in your mouth when you forgot Henry Fonda was dead."

Hey Bob. Where's the scotch?

You'll have to forgive me. I'm a huge Henry Fonda fan, I'd just watched him on laser disc, and I'd totally forgotten he'd died a few years earlier. Although Henry Fonda will always be alive for me, my question kind of killed the moment.

Jane: If I didn't say I was sorry then, I'll say it now. Sorry. Very sorry.

*

Back to reality. I sense someone getting near, someone who will have the courage to go for the close encounter. Suddenly an old feeling sets in: loneliness. Odd emotion, but that's what happens. Tim Dick is about to dissolve. Tim Allen will take his place, and I don't have any control over it.

A woman, about forty, standing fifteen feet away, turns on a big smile. My Tim Allen grin automatically flashes in return. She doesn't move, so I smile again, turn away and walk to the nearby coffee bar for a donut and a jolt. Low blood sugar, remember. Suddenly the lady is at my side.

"You know what?" she says.

"No. What?"

"You look just like that guy on *Home Improvement.*"

"You . . . think so?"

She pauses, transfixed. "Damn, even the voice! You know that guy on *Home Improvement*?"

"Um, um, Tim, uh, Allen?" I realize that she doesn't think I'm me. This could be fun.

"Yeah! You look like him, kinda. Your voice is really close to his, but his face is a little thinner. And I think he's taller. Yeah, he's a lot taller, and you're a little stockier. And he looks a lot younger, but God, other than that . . . And your hair is a different color."

"Well, we are what God made us," I say, with a shrug and a good-natured smile. It's not turning out to be that much fun.

"Damn! I'd say it *was* you if I didn't know better."

My donuts and coffee arrive.

"Could I have some cream, please?"

"Say 'cream' again. Just do that," says the woman.

"Cream."

"It sounds. . . . I should get my sister. If we fooled her, she would think that you're that guy. What's your name?"

"Fred."

"Fred, this is so fun. Do this for me: bark."

So, just like on the show, I go, "Arugh? R-r-r."

"That is just unbelievable! This is just great." And she runs off to get her sister.

Now is my chance to escape. I've already forgotten what I wanted when I came in here. I grab a pizza from the freezer case on the way up front. But when I get there I see it's impossible. There are long lines at each check stand. I'd be trapped, a sitting duck on the opening day of hunting season.

Even if I get in the cash-only line for people with less than 10 items, I can't guarantee a quick getaway. There's always that person with a shopping cart full of stuff who says, "I've got 17 cuts of meat, but it's all *meat*. Does that count as one?" Personally, I think just the question alone counts as one.

I could put a shopping bag on my head, but then people might mistake me for the Unknown Comic or a stock boy gone awry. Either way, I ditch the pizza and exit.

Just outside I nearly trip over a panhandler sitting on the sidewalk. He looks up at me with a glint of recognition. I know the look. He thinks he knows me — people who see me on TV often believe we're already intimate. Wait a minute. That's weird. If he can afford a TV, what's he begging for? You know, what's even weirder is that I think I've seen him before, too. But I don't know any other homeless guys except for the one earlier with the Indian blanket . . . this one's with a dog, but . . . Geez. I'm not sure what to do. Should I say something? Keep walking? And then he says, "You know you have the answer, don't cha?"

"Answer?"

"It's in the eggs."

Oh my god, the egg thing again . . .

"I don't know what you're talking about," I say, quickly stuffing a twenty into his cup.

"You look thinner on TV," he calls out.

This is definitely not the same guy who distracted me this morning and nearly caused my traffic accident . . . and yet . . . Now I'm nervous. What's going on? This kind of stuff is not supposed to happen. What is there, some homeless guy's union? Did they talk about me at a meeting and decide to have some fun at my expense? And what's with the egg thing? Are these guys secretly taking money from the California Egg Council or something? I'd rather discover that this is an hallucination because I took Spot's medicine this morning instead of my own. At least that would make more sense.

Maybe I should just drive around for a while until I calm down and get a grip on things.

*

I'VE DECIDED THE SITUATION is not worth getting crazy over. That leaves one more thing that bothers me: The lady in the market who said I looked like "Tim Allen" on TV.

What does that mean in terms of my identity? I *am* him, I just don't look that way in public. I'm also not him, because, of course, TV always adds 10-15 pounds. To a guy going through mid-life intro-spection — which is basically a deep identity crisis of sorts — this is like grapefruit juice in a paper cut: It gets your attention.

There's nothing unusual about a man wondering about who and even what he is. Granted, it's usually a professor of philosophy doing well below the speed limit in his ten-year-old Volvo, an indi-gent on a park bench, savoring a Sterno cocktail, or the actor who played the Beast in *Beauty and the Beast* — and hasn't worked much since. But not me. Yet lately I *have* been asking the big ques-tions: "Who am I?," "Why am I here?," and "How come the psychic hotline didn't already know I'd be calling?"

(However, Laura says these are better questions than, "Who dialed all these 976 numbers on the phone bill?")

Who's me *is* the question, isn't it? It's been on my mind since I awoke this morning, and frankly I'm getting a little jammed up trying to figure it out.

Well: I'm one human being. Yet there are two distinct aspects of my identity, two different forms of me, so to speak: TV Tim and real life Tim, and . . . wait a minute. This reminds me of something I read in one of my physics books about wave/particle duality: subatomic *particles*, all of which are referred to as quanta — sounds like the name of a new model Chrysler — are said to *also* exist as waves. Where things really get weird is that these quanta don't have to exist as *either* wave or particle exclusively, but both can occur at the *same time.*

This is not only the basic paradox of quantum physics, it's one of the most mysterious and magical facts about reality ever revealed, next to the Michael Jackson/Lisa Marie Presley wedding.

But how could that be? The simple definition of a particle is something contained in one place. It has a definite location. A wave is spread out all over the place. Picture a large rock jutting out of the ocean. You can imagine it speckled with sea gull droppings if you're into detail. The rock represents a particle and of course, the ocean waves play themselves. It doesn't seem to make sense that quanta — let's call them subatomic events — could be the metaphorical rock and the ocean *simultaneously*. But the amazing thing is that the billion zillion quadrillion particles that make up the rock *do* have a "wave nature," just like ocean waves. Still, I wouldn't want to surf the rock.

The obverse is also true: Stuff we know to be wavelike in nature, like light, *also* behaves like a particle.

I'm not crazy. This was all proven long ago when Einstein, the Minnesota Fats of physics, played billiards with an atom and knocked off one of its electrons with a neat little bank shot using a *particle* of light (which is supposed to be a wave, right), called a "photon" as a cue ball. Unfortunately, the shot also sank the eight ball early and he immediately lost the game in which, I believe, he was competing against God. Disgusted, Einstein gave up pool and decided instead to play dice with the Universe.

So how does this all apply to me? Suddenly it's obvious. The real life Tim is the particle, and TV Tim is the wave.

When "Tim Allen" appears on your TV at home, he gets there by being turned into electromagnetic waves that spread out all over the place, are picked up by your TV antenna (or transmitted over your cable), and even travel deep into outer space. These waves travel at light speed, or 186,000 miles per second. Despite this incredible speed, *Home Improvement* probably won't be in any alien's TV guide for many years to come, due to the fantastic distances involved. In fact, scientists say that if intelligent life does exist in any nearby star system, they would just now be receiving TV and radio signals from the 50s. This means they should be watching the *Ed Sullivan Show* next Sunday night, and may well think all men on earth ride unicycles while juggling to impress their girlfriends named, "Rama-Lama-Ding-Dong." I just hope when they finally get to see the movie *Independence Day* they don't get any crazy ideas.

The flip side of this classic duality — that waves are also particles — is natural, too. When I'm driving and some idiot suddenly cuts me off and maybe flips me the bird, I have instant bad feelings and thoughts, like reflex-fear and murder. These thoughts and feelings can be seen as brain waves on an electroencephalograph. (I recently had one installed in my car. Did I mention that I am a high-tech gadget freak? I'm hoping to get the guidance system from the space shuttle Atlantis for Christmas.) These brain waves are almost *instantly* converted into adrenaline molecules — that is, particles. Fortunately, I don't act on my irate impulses, since this could land me once again in prison, where a man truly fits the definition of a particle, as mentioned earlier: something confined in one place.

I'm starting to feel *really* good. I now see how basic and natural this double identity duality thing really is. Being both Tim Allen, the celebrity, and Tim Dick, the real life guy, doesn't seem so confusing and strange. "Duality" is just the way things are on our level of existence. Here's how I know: I can be the real Tim Dick, out shopping, and be on someone's TV at the same time. It all fits!

Which reminds me: A wise man once said, "enlightenment is the acceptance of the way things are." I guess I could take a cue from the rock I mentioned earlier. It accepts its double existence with nonchalance. I think I should be at least as enlightened as a rock.

*

O H J E E Z, look at the time. I've just been driving around aimlessly and I'm running behind schedule — not that I have anything particular to do except run a couple more errands and find the hood ornament when I get home.

At the cleaner, a young man examines my receipt and shakes his head.

"Not ready yet."

"My wife dropped it off Thursday. This is Saturday. It's been two days."

"So?"

"Well, it's been two days. This is a One-Hour Cleaners."

"That's just the name of the place."

"What do you mean, it's just the name of the place?"

"It's a brand name. One-Hour Cleaners."

"So what's next," I say, a bit on edge. "A restaurant called All You Can Eat for a Dollar?"

"Actually it's called Free Food."

"So just because something has a name, doesn't mean it necessarily has anything to do with what it really is?"

"What it really is, sir, is a restaurant chain. The company just opened one two blocks to the west. Try it, I think you'll like it. They take all major credit cards."

"Funny. Now when can I pick up my clothes?"

"Your cleaning will be ready Monday, sir."

"You mean two days from now?"

"Next Monday."

"Two days from now. I just have to be sure what you mean."

"Georgian or Julian calendar?"

He hands me the receipt with a smile. Laura's going to be ticked that I didn't get our stuff — but I can't believe she doesn't know how weird this place is. She comes here all the time.

*

W HATEVER I EXPECT to happen today, doesn't. I need something predictable to center me. That means three small hamburgers, large fries, and a Coke. I'm going to McDonald's.

I don't want to go inside and repeat what happened at the supermarket, so I'll have to forego the McDonald's Playland and use the drive-through line. It's safer. There're a few cars ahead of me, but not many. The wait shouldn't be long.

Finally, the woman in the car ahead finishes ordering and pulls out of sight.

"Welcome to McDonald's. May I take your order please?"

"Uh, yeah."

"Wait. Let me guess."

"Guess? What is this, a new promotion? What do you win? Left over Disney Hunchback Dolls? Power Ranger paraphernalia?"

"Just let me guess. You already know the answers. Please."

"Okay. What do I want?"

"Three little hamburgers, large fries, and a Coke."

Amazing. He knew exactly what I wanted.

"Nope. Wrong."

"Am not."

"Alright. How'd you know?"

"Some people are easy to read. They put it right out there for you. They don't hide it."

"Is that so? Maybe you can tell me what I had for breakfast."

"Trick question, sir. Didn't eat any."

"And you can tell all this through the microphone?"

"Yup."

"You might look into working for Kenny Kingston's Psychic Friends Network. Probably pays more. Oh, but then you must already know that."

Maybe those homeless guys were looking for this guy. He seems to be the one with all the answers.

"That'll be $5.43. Pay at the first window, please."

"Hey, wait a minute." But there's no response.

At the pay window, the guy with the headphone smiles at me.

"Hello, Mr. Allen. Didn't mean to upset you. I just remembered you from before. Thought it was weird that you ordered three little burgers." Then he points to a wide-angle mirror that allows him to see when a car pulls up to the menu.

"Well, you scared the hell out of me. Don't do it again."

He keeps smiling and I calm down. I realize he didn't mean anything bad by it.

"You have a little girl, don't you?" he asks.

"Yes, I do. Do you have kids?"

"In a way."

His voice soothes me. I don't recognize the guy, but once again I get the sense that I know him. This has, of course, been happening all day. At least this guy has a job instead of an empty cup or an Indian blanket. But what does he mean that he has kids "in a way"?

Behind me, a couple horns blare.

"I'd better go," I say. He takes my money and I drive slowly to the pickup window where my order is waiting.

I'VE MADE IT HOME SAFELY without endangering the public. Spot's waiting inside. She knows I'm the only one around, so she'll follow me until she gets what she wants most — love. I pet her, put away my "dinner," turn on the TV, pet her some more, and spoon out her dinner. I'm not in a great mood. The day is almost over, I haven't found what I'm looking for, I'm still confused by so many things, and I'm bone tired. And frustrated. It's all coming down on me at once: the detachment, the malaise, the missing car part. These are the moments when I wish I *wasn't* really here. I guess I'll just sit quietly and watch Spot gobble her Tender Vittles, and try not to breathe in the aroma.

Suddenly I remember that I haven't checked my E-mail all day. Quickly, I'm in the office, booting the computer, logging on.

"Welcome," the service says. "You've got mail."

I like that guy's voice. He's so darn enthusiastic — never unhappy. So dependable. Unless the system is down.

It's always exciting to get mail, unless it's computer junk mail, which I really wish they'd do something about. I have only one message from someone named TAO/MAN.

Who's that?

Guess I'd better click on the mailbox icon and find out. Wow — here's what the e-mail says:

"Dear Tim,

Things are not what they seem, and yet they are. There's a secret no one's telling you, that you already know. But don't worry. You aren't the only one thinking about this. Don't look for the answers. Be the answer.

Happiness,

TAO/MAN."

Holy shit!

SEVEN

TAO/MAN?

I get the obvious connection. I've been thinking a lot about physics, Buddha, and the nature of beer, but I can't help thinking that this meeting of TAO/MAN and TOOLMAN — which is my on-screen name — is not simply a coincidence. Let's just call it "synchronicity," a word coined by the famous psychologist and philosopher, Carl Jung. He defined synchronicity as a *meaningful* coincidence; a significantly related pattern of chance.

And here's a really synchronous fact: Jung coined the term synchronicity while lecturing in London about the Tao.

The question I have is how did that *individual*, the TAO/MAN, know what I was thinking? He did, for God's sake, know what I was thinking! Is it possible he's tapping my phone and watching me from across the street with high-powered binoculars, gathering scandalous info for "The Globe"? Or do people on the same journey simply share the same mental wavelength. "TOOLMAN to TAO/MAN, breaker, breaker."

Mind reading *is* possible. I know because it happened to me.

One night, about 20 years ago, when I was in college, a friend of mine and I sat together for three hours and talked. Only we didn't move our mouths or say any words.

I know it sounds crazy. It's the kind of thing you can't tell just anyone without seeming like the guy who claims he's seen a UFO. Well, it happened. I know we spoke mind to mind. The guy I was with knows who he is, and he knows that even today, when we meet, that evening always comes up in our conversation. Every time, he says, "That was the weirdest night of my life. But I don't want to talk about it anymore."

"But it happened, right?" I say?

"Yes, it happened. Now will you drop it?"

It wasn't weird, it was glorious. I wish I could figure out what we did and do it again.

Here's what happened: We were watching television. Well, not exactly watching. It was just on. There was a candle. Incense. The J. Geils Band blasting on the stereo. We were drinking beer. Every sensory portal was accounted for.

I ended up getting really involved in the candle flame. I let it take me places. Things got very disjointed. I pretty much lost all notion of who I was, but didn't have any problem with it. The further out I got, the better I liked it. I felt so involved in the moment that it must have scared my friend because suddenly I heard his voice yelling for me to come back. I heard his voice as though I was drowning. Or dying.

"Come back. Come back!"

I looked right at him while he yelled this, but his mouth wasn't moving. I thought/said, "What?!" Apparently my mouth didn't move either.

He thought/said, "How do you feel? Come back. I'm worried."

I thought/said, "Do you realize you're not moving your lips?"

He went, "You're not either."

I thought/said, "I'm not?"

He said: "What?" That startled us because it was the first word we had actually heard.

Afterwards we tried every which way to figure it out.

I later experimented with this technique in class. I tried to influence my professors to give me good grades.

"Please," I thought/said/begged, "I need an A."

Didn't work, of course. Maybe I should have brought a candle to classes, but I think it was against fire regulations.

I joke now, but this really happened and it was a watershed moment in my life. I began to believe that there was more "out there" than my "reality" included. I started to read metaphysics and look into myself. What I didn't do is figure out a way to talk about this experience to anyone, until now.

*

THE TRUTH, OF COURSE, is that what concerned me then, and now, has apparently long been on many people's minds. We all come to it in our own way and in our own time. Mankind has always sought answers; asking questions defines our humanity. We are the universe, aware and questioning itself. And these days we seem to want resolution more than ever. Maybe it's because as we approach January 1, 2001 — the end of the millennium — we are naturally filled with the need for renewal and change. One epoch ends, and another begins. We're in transit.

I don't know how else to explain the outpouring of spiritual bestsellers that purport to show us the path to enlightenment, self-esteem, and how to shed unwanted pounds while we sleep. It seems that at this time in history the human race, like me, is going through its own mid-life identity crisis, seeking to redefine itself in its relation to God, the universe — and itself. Whether we care to admit it or not, we're all on some kind of search. We want to know how to live right. We want to know how to die right. We want to know if it's okay to make a right turn on a red in the Afterworld.

I'm looking for something, too: A way to overcome the detachment and feel reconnected to life, at midlife. A way to feel good about myself more of the time. A way to accept the love given me. A way to love God — whatever/whoever that is.

And who knows, while I'm at it I might even come up with a Unified Field Theory, or at least a cure for my insomnia.

The synchronistic significance of TAO/MAN's name is not lost on me, either. After having spent many years (in a previous life) as a missionary in China, I know that literally translated from the Chinese, "Tao" means "the way." In other words, the deep nature and guiding principle of creation itself. The true law of God. The perfect micro-brewery beer.

The typical Toolman would call it "how things work."

I also know that when one speaks Chinese, one must be careful with pronunciation because a slight change in emphasis gives you TAOU, which I understand is actually a gecko lizard dish popular in Mongolia. (Add a dollop of plum sauce and it tastes just like free range dog.)

Let's assume TAO/MAN's for real. I'm not surprised that someone else intercepted the intense vibrations that must be emanating from my head. My wife would say misery loves company, and it actually makes some scientific sense. Brain waves are electromagnetic in nature and like radio and TV signals, they must travel through the air. If not, then we'd have to wonder if our craniums are lined with tinfoil, leaving potent brain waves to ricochet around inside our skull cases. Excluding my immediate family, I don't buy that. I figure tapping into someone's thoughts is no more difficult than listening to a "supposedly" private cell phone call with a police scanner — as long as you're set up to receive and interpret what you get. However, getting mentally set up to do this may entail spending twenty years in a Tibetan monastery, in total silence, staring at a piece of rice. Women, on the other hand, seem born with the ability to read men's minds. And then use it against us.

(Which reminds me: How come Laura hasn't tried to call back? I hope the girls are all right. Bears can be aggressive. Ah, so can women. I'm sure they're fine.)

If brain waves can travel beyond our heads without need of a huge antenna dish and leased transponder space on a communications satellite, it also makes sense that we don't end with our skins. I've read about this idea before. One guy who put it in a way anyone could understand is the late philosopher, Alan Watts. His specialty was interpreting Eastern religious/spiritual thought for Western audiences. In one of his radio broadcasts called "Death and Rebirth," Watts said:

"We think we end with our skins. And it's manifestly provable that we don't. Whatever is going on inside the skin is inseparable from atmosphere, temperature, food energies, microbes — all kinds of things going on outside the skin. We can't live without that. Therefore, where do you draw the line?"

Good question. He tried to illustrate the answer with a different example.

"How big is the sun? How are you going to define the sun? By where it's visible fires end? You could define the sun as the entire reach of its heat. Or the entire reach of its light, in which case the galaxy would be inside the sun. Thus, you can define yourself by the entire reach of your consciousness, in which case the galaxy is in your mind. So are the other galaxies. Where are you going to draw the line?"

No wonder I can't get any sleep. Obviously, the universe is in my head and I didn't even know it. I hope this doesn't mean there are beings in some parallel universe rewiring my brain circuitry for more power. Wouldn't that be the ultimate irony.

I wish there were a simple explanation for the odd E-mail, but it was addressed directly to me, TOOLMAN. As much as I want to resist the implications, I know TAO/MAN's message means I should wake up and pay attention. This happened before when I bought the hood ornament, when I had my tarot cards read, and when the Roto Rooter guy said, "I think it's only a soft blockage."

In each case what I discovered is that . . . nothing is what it seems.

I suppose the thing to do now is to watch events carefully, figure out meanings, notice unlikely coincidence, see if patterns emerge, and remember that vertical stripes always make you look slimmer.

*

I WANT TO WATCH two Sci-fi movies before I go to bed. That always helps me rest. I love science fiction; it takes my mind away from my everyday concerns and puts it on future concerns. Some people like romance novels, I like cheesy aliens and shiny metallic objects.

Wait. What's that? I heard something. There it is again. Better turn down the TV. No, it's not tinkling bells. It was a scurrying. Jesus, there it is again. It's amazing how your heart beat can go from a resting rate to 160 beats per minute without you even moving a muscle. Anyway, I think the noise is coming from above. Something's definitely in the attic or on the roof.

This has happened before. The last time, tree rats got into the attic through a broken vent screen. The noise was incredibly annoying. First we heard the chewing, which rats do constantly. You see, their teeth keep growing, and the chewing is Nature's way to keep the teeth from getting too large. Then it seemed like they were holding rat Olympics, sprinting from one side of the attic to the other. They did all the events, from vaulting to the uneven bars. Worst of all, they ran the rat races at around 3:15 in the morning.

I'd better investigate. Not because I want to, but because I'm a man. It's required by virtue of my gender.

*

I USE THE ATTIC to store things like old stereo boxes. Laura hates that, and she does have a point. The boxes are empty. I keep them because the instructions always say you need the original packaging in case you have to send back the unit. That's a pretty fatalistic approach to product development, but I follow directions when it comes to electronics.

My attic access is a pull-down stair. I reluctantly grab hold of the string far above my head, open the door, and bring the ladder down. In my head I heard a Bernard Herman score played by discordant violins. This is where I imagine either my worst childhood monster nightmare springing to life, or my most dreaded, fatal household accident happening. (You know, 80% of accidents happen in the home!) I can just picture it: one foot on the steps, the other foot going into the attic. I hoist myself up, grab the wrong thing, get a nice jolt of electricity, and fall backwards, down the ladder, plummeting to the floor. Unlike Chevy Chase, I don't get back up and mutter an amusing witticism. Instead, I'm cold all weekend and smell very bad by Sunday, when my family returns. They walk in just as I expire, and the last words I hear are Laura yelling, "God it stinks! Tim? Have you been cooking Bratwurst again?"

So far I've been very careful.

Getting into the attic is dangerous, but the risks don't end once inside. For instance I always have to remember to — *ouch!* — bend over so I don't conk my head on the first beam.

Geez that hurt! God I hate doing that. I did this once in France, in the basement of an old house on a vineyard. The ceiling was low and made of rock. Scraping the skin off the top of my head was so painful that I actually dropped to my knees, grabbed a bottle of vintage wine, opened it, and drank a whole bunch before I fell over. I stayed drunk the rest of the day, in spite of my host's revulsion. Or so I'm told. By the next morning I'd totally forgotten about my wound until I brushed my hair and reminded myself. Fortunately, because of my self-induced hangover, the pain was only intermittent, and I had the occasional moment of clarity in which I marveled at this fine example of life's clever checks and balances.

My grandmother used to say, "You never scrape your head once, but three times." Thanks, Grandma. Head scrapes are bad, but I believe there are two other devastating ways to hurt yourself — and I hope they don't come in threes. One is catching the little toe on a chair leg while moving swiftly, which I skillfully accomplished this morning. The other is kneeling on a bolt. A bolt on the patella is a real killer. You always hit that tender part of your knee that feels like it can't be repaired by modern miracle surgical techniques. So you must bear the pain. To do this, grit your teeth, hold your breath, and get a bit dizzy. The miracle is that it most always goes away, unless you get too dizzy and fall and hurt yourself again. However, "Attaboys!" to whomever spent all that time at the blackboard designing the human body. Very clever!

The attic is a tricky place. To move around up here I have to walk down the center of a beam. I focus hard and think of Nadia Comaneci, and gracefully place one foot in front of the other, smiling at the judges when possible.

On each side is deep insulation. The pink fiberglass may seem solid, but if you take a wrong step your leg becomes a chandelier — and inevitably, points are deducted.

Now that I'm up here, I can see that after the earthquake we stored more than mere empty boxes. Maybe the hood ornament is up here. I don't see how, but when you're looking for something, you often find it exactly where and when you least expect it.

Maybe I'm in for a big surprise. But first I must concentrate on sticking my dismount.

D ID I MENTION that the whole place smells like mothballs? Have you ever smelled mothballs? If so, how did you get their tiny little legs apart? Sorry. Dumb little joke leftover from childhood. The odor is so vile that it not only keeps moths away but causes un-sheared sheep on the other side of the world to bleat inconsolably. I don't think you can get rid of the smell without airing out the clothes for six months in a hurricane wind. I'm sure it's not good for people, which is why scientists invented cedar closet lining.

There's so much stuff piled up here. There's my old photography portfolio. I have some great shots inside. Unfortunately, the box was in a flood at my mom's house, and all my best films from high school and college spent a year in a puddle. Now everything's water-stained, yellow, and stuck together. So why keep them? Simple. I'm a firm believer in technology and I'm convinced that in the future, scientists using holographic wizardry will be able to regenerate whole images from the pieces of the flood-damaged negatives. If not, I'm confident that I can convince critics that I worked hard to achieve that look from the get-go. It's such a comforting thought that Art has no boundaries.

My grandpa's old Bolex camera is in another box. He was the nicest guy in the world. I really loved him. When I was younger he would ask me and my brothers, "You guys want to see my slides?"

Hell, yes.

These weren't just any slides. Today I'd call them gentle, provocative pictures. Topless models in ample bikinis. The bottoms went above their navels and they were always holding something over their head. They were, in effect, saying, "Look at my breasts, kid. No big deal. You have a lot to look forward to, but there's a lot of mystery left, too."

Gotta love Grandpa.

This reminds me of something that happened after my first

book was published. In it I wrote about how my pubescent awakening was jump-started by Playboy Playmate Ellen Stratton's centerfold when I was about 11 years old. After *Naked Man* came out I got a nice letter from Ellen's daughter. She'd given her mom the book. Ellen was delighted I'd remembered her so vividly . . . er, fondly. However, she didn't include a current photo because she said she didn't want to alter my memories of her. A kind and courteous gesture.

I also see three huge boxes of correspondence I received from all my friends when I was in prison. I kept every letter. Some were very funny. Although I haven't read them since, I save them because they're a part of me. Too bad they also got wet in the flood. Perhaps someday Kady will open these boxes and say, "Wow, wood pulp." Or maybe, since the energy of the universe is in constant motion, the subatomic particles of these now brittle bits of stationery will swirl around and around and reconstitute themselves into letters no one's read before.

What is this attic if not a memory vault, a physical reproduction of my brain full of memories, all boxed up and categorized?

I hold on to memories because it reminds me where I've been. I try to learn from my history and not repeat old mistakes. I've made some real "Let's-buy-a-summer-home-in-Chernobyl-level" winners. But I believe that by applying this old Hindu saying: "I use my memories; I don't let my memories use me," I ultimately benefit.

Okay, it sounded good.

It's great to remember happy, pleasant and meaningful times, but bad memories are there too. I can recall intense feelings of confinement, fear, torture, and brutality; but who wants to remember the first grade? That's the problem. It's hard to edit memories unless you're a politician. Then it's a career.

Scientists say, of all the five senses, the sense of smell can trigger the most vivid and detailed memories. This is probably a holdover from our caveman days when fresh deer droppings meant "lunch is close by," and, unfortunately, the smell of saber tooth tiger dung meant "bummer." I know this works for me, since just the smell of an old National Geographic Magazine can bring back vivid memories of my first sexual experience.

Memories seem to define The "I" within us. Our basic ego/personality is fashioned and moderated by memories, but are they *us*? In a way, yes. Could one function without them? Sure because, in another way, memories seem no more than a steamer trunk of images, reactions, sensations, and the rest, that we drag around for a lifetime. Suppose you didn't have memories? Then you'd have amnesia. Now suppose you have amnesia. Aside from the pain of loved ones who miss you, and forgetting that you're allergic to bees, it's no big deal. You simply start again, living life and creating new memories. You don't actually need all those old memories.

This makes me take what I said a while ago — that there is no "I" inside us — one step further: If memories define our ego/person-ality, but it's possible to substitute one set of memories for another, as in the case of amnesia, then it seems that all we are, are points of view. So the important question is, "Who is doing the looking? Who is the 'I' now?"

I have no blessed idea.

Whatever the role of memory, I think the best thing to shoot for is to live in the moment. Put one way or another, we've heard this our entire lives. Stop and smell the roses. Life is what happens while you're making other plans. Be here now. Bottom line, the idea is the common thread of many philosophies, religions, and mystical paths.

Too bad it's not that easy to do. People have devoted lifetimes to pursuing that elusive goal, commonly described as Nirvana, or a state of unity with the oneness. And when they get there they finally understand this: Living in the moment is not something we have to exert one drop of effort to do. *You already are in the moment.* You can't be anywhere else. Being in the moment, but obsessing about the past, or what might or might not happen in the future — that's where so many of us unnecessarily deplete our energy, not to mention our pockets by investing in stocks and bonds.

The challenge seems to be *experiencing* the "now." This seems simply a matter of perception. I think this can be proven just by thinking about the brain. Information about what's happening comes in and is processed. This takes time — a minuscule amount of time, but time nonetheless. So there's a lag between an experience and the brain recognizing it. The chemical reaction of sensory processing and thought takes place in the present but the results, when read and although experienced as contemporary — are already the past.

Suddenly I feel like I'm living inside a seven-second tape delay.

Fortunately our perceptions come quickly enough to seem cohesive and continuous. Life is like watching an IMAX film that runs at 70 frames per second and feels so much more real than the films at your local multiplex that run at 35 frames per second. And for $7.50 a pop, it had better be good.

As impossible as experiencing the moment may seem, this is still the goal of many Eastern religions because the realizations that occur on the path actually *do* affect you and change the way you experience every moment ever after. Suddenly, you are freed from the pain and limitation of the past, and the fear and uncertainty of the future. Your attitude toward life changes and your delayed experiences of "the moment" increasingly incline toward a state of grace. Am I beginning to glow right now?

This doesn't mean we can simply do without memories. For instance, I wouldn't want to forget the names of my wife and child, or the automatic teller pin code — which I think I just forgot. And if, as a child, I stuck my hand (thinking it was a marshmallow) into a fire, I would hope to apply that experience to the next time I sat by a fire. It's a rather tricky balance.

Memories define us, but they're not us. Retained and processed well, they create wisdom. Incorrectly handled, they create confusion and misplaced expectation. I'd go on if I could remember more of what I've read about this subject. Let me put it this way: Our memory-built personality may just not be our truest self. That's why I do all this late-night reading. I'm looking for my truest self, or at least a damn good explanation of why there's no good explanation.

Wait. I hear that noise again. I mean, I *heard* that noise again. At least it *seems* like I hear it now, but now we know differently. There will be a test on this next Tuesday.

The noise seems to be coming from the far end of the attic. To follow it I've got to crawl along a rafter toward where the roof slope meets the cross beams. A 2.5 degree of difficulty. There's a stack of old artwork in my way. I know this pile. Most are drawings I didn't like well enough to put in my permanent art portfolio. Come to think of it, where *is* my portfolio? I recall seeing it in at my mother's house during the last Christmas gathering, but I know it didn't get damaged in the flood. So I brought it to California and . . . that's where I lose track. The portfolio is very important to me because it contains all my best artwork from the time I was a kid to when I went to art classes. There are neat logos, cartoon characters, car designs, blueprints, paintings, and all my designs in my head that spilled out on to paper, along with some stains from lunches I will never forget.

I wish that having a sense of design was a part of everybody's life, and yet . . . Laura and I will often be out in the car, see a structure, and say, "Now, how did *that* get built? There's some real ugly stuff out there. Where are the design police when you need them?" But nonetheless, it was someone's idea, spilled out in to concrete, and hardened there until the next earthquake. Not that I'm wishing for another any time soon.

Good design is not really subjective. Design is composed of elements: form, function, symmetry, balance, harmony, composition, color, scale. Great elements eh? Mix them well and wonderful things happen. Or you get the Edsel. Either way, I call design "applied art."

I've always loved art and design. Industrial designers like Brooks Stephens were my heroes. He did toasters and outboard motors. It wasn't high-end, art school stuff, but it was hip. He had fun with it. These are the guys who designed the modern washing machine. Once it was a big brown machine in the basement. Someone realized it would be easier to sell if you could see what was inside. So they added a round window and made them white. Form follows function. Then some people overlay style. The early American cars covered their lack of inventiveness with style. But style, to me, is the worst part of design. A good design lasts a long time.

*

I'VE GOT TO MOVE these boxes to get into the corner. Just put these papers over here and . . . hey, there's a big folder underneath.

I'll be damned. It's my art portfolio. I can't believe it. I found the thing! It's a little blue sky victory in a pretty dreary day. But what's this picture? I don't remember doing this. It's a drawing of a huge rock plateau — a Venezuelan Tepui. Did I do this?

There's that noise again. It's coming from the other side of the attic now. If I can get. . . . Ow! Dammit. My head. That's twice.

Now the only noise I hear is the ringing in my head. Whatever else I heard is gone, it's over. I'm taking the portfolio down to my office to put it away. Just gotta turn around and . . . "Yow!!!" That's three. Grandma, are you happy now? That really hurts. I slammed my forehead into a two-by-four. Whoa. I'd better sit down for a minute. Grit the teeth. Hold the breath. I've got tiny supernovas popping in the corners of my eyes. Wow. Look at those dust motes everywhere, floating through the beams of the sunset coming through the main attic vent. This stuff is in the air all the time but we never think about it. Maybe this is what it's really like in the "nothingness" between the stars, or between the atoms of a solid object.

I'm a little dizzy. This looks like a strong carton to lean against. There's some writing on the side. It reads: Philosophy Books. These are my college philosophy texts. Isn't fate relentless? I kept them, thinking that one day I might go back and try reading them again, but I haven't. The problem is that in school the philosophy we studied was so dry and devoid of life that it seemed so much word play. There was no place for our instincts about the nature of things. But the more I read in *The Tao of Physics* about Eastern thought and Western science being on a collision course, the more I believe there must soon be a new philosophy created which will lead thinkers beyond the literal and logical to the intuitive.

I think I had to live a while to figure that out. And there goes memory experience outweighing "in the moment."

Is there no reality except that which you create for yourself? Does everything depend on one's point of view? Is it all a matter of letting go of absolutes and accepting more perspectives? If so, then the really interesting part happens when our perspective suddenly changes.

Think of the fish cartoon in the magazine that fell on my head in the garage. One fish asks the other fish about "this thing called water." Water is their world. It's all around them. They don't even know they're wet. There's probably fifty words for "seaweed" in Fishspeak, but not one for "wet." Water is not only literally transparent but not part of their normal level of consciousness. It's beyond their perception . . . until they get caught.

And then it's too late. Think about being jerked *out* of the water, only to see the earth, trees, sky, sun (the white light?), and some giant monster with a pole in one hand, and a Budweiser in the other. First, you can't breathe, and then you die too quickly to have any chance to appreciate the revelation that there is much more to the world than you suspected. Your only comfort is expiring in a basket filled with other fish, something you *do* know. There may be a few seconds to whisper, "What the hell's going on?" but the chances of an answer — much less a coherent one — are about as slim as bumping into Mother Teresa at a Madonna concert.

However, sometimes a fishermen will throw back a fish. Whether or not this is a lucky circumstance is uncertain. Armed with a new point of view about the universe, the fish might be better off in a frying pan. Apparently a tossed-back fish is either killed or ignored by the other fish because who wants to listen to incessant babbling about the big hook, the clear blue sky, and the horrible drunken creature who fondled you? Sure, from *our* point of view, it seems like the other fish should listen and learn and, if they've really grasped what's happening, avoid the big hook if they know what's good for them. But then we're not fish.

But are we much smarter? We hear stories like these. Sometimes they're told by a guy with three parents (Mary, Joseph, and God), or by a farmer who claims to have taken a spaceship ride with little green men, or by a bearded yogi from Calcutta who says we can levitate if we try, or by a quantum physicist whose science has only strengthened his spirituality. Do *we* listen?

Do you suppose that this little fish story might also explain what happens to humans who have near-death experiences. Although there's no "apparent" lunge for bait involved, maybe when we die we're just being pulled out of our natural environment into one that *includes* our world but has a few major extra dimensions as well. And there's God, holding a halogen lamp, chugging an Amstel Lite. (My brand!)

Now forget death for a moment. Humans can also have this perspective-changing experience without having to worry about leaving before they get to start spending their retirement savings. I'm speaking of the experience of enlightenment. Sort of like laughing at a joke, or burning your fingers on a hot hood ornament, having an orgasm, or being abducted by aliens. In some cases the "wow" passes very quickly. In others circumstances there are deep body cavity probes to endure. And then there are the aliens. (Why must aliens always probe?) But it happens, and it leaves behind a residue that changes you. Then like a fish, we're thrown back.

I think a lot of people we believe are strange have just been thrown back. We see them on daytime talk shows.

If it happened to you, what would you tell your friends. Would they even listen? What would you tell yourself?

This much I know now: My growling stomach tells me it's time to go back down to the house and eat those burgers and fries.

EIGHT

WHEN I MAKE a commitment, I keep it. That's why, ever since I climbed down from the attic three hours ago, I have wandered through the house searching for the hood ornament with the relentless determination of a shark who must either keep swimming or sink to the bottom and die. It's sad that wanting something so badly does not guarantee that you get it, or I would have found my missing car part hours ago, not to mention, had a date back in high school with "Miss October." Sharks have much better luck.

Good thing the day has not been entirely wasted. If nothing else, I've managed to do something completely different than usual. Oh, it's been frustrating. But let's look on the bright side: because of this tedious search for the hood ornament, I have been able to reflect upon the many and often neglected aspects of my life: family, friends, my daughter, love, goals, and process. And it's always fun to twist my brain around a quantum physics concept or two. The only thing more challenging than reading this stuff is remembering it.

Of course, there's no way I'm going to waste one second of my Sunday doing the same thing!

Before I go to sleep tonight I have to find the hood ornament. When you misplace something that you know damn well shouldn't be missing in the first place, it drives you completely nuts until you find it. The missing hood ornament is an itch that I can't scratch. It's like meeting someone I've known for years and suddenly blanking on their name.

Only much, much worse — like waving back at someone who isn't waving at you.

The only place I haven't looked is in my bedroom.

*

FIRST, LET ME level with you. My bed is queen-sized, not king. But that's okay. I feel secure enough with my own masculinity to go queen, and besides, I've got a petite wife and we like to snuggle. But lately I think Laura wishes we had separate bedrooms because I snore — at least that's what I'm told. I've never heard it once. Anyway, I tried snore pillows. Didn't work. My wife tried her version of snore pillows, which seemed a little too much like suffocation. Didn't work. I tried hypnosis. Worked for her: Every time Laura snapped her fingers I fed the dog. I thought about trying the new patch that you tape across the bridge of your nose, but how's that going to help? Shouldn't you tape it over your *nostrils*?

Now, Laura and I don't sleep together anymore. We're still in the same bed, but when she's sleeping, I'm awake, and vice versa. The only good thing is that I get to watch Laura sleep, which I love doing. She says she also likes to watch me sleep — something about a secret fantasy.

"Yeah Tim, watching you sleep helps me foster this wild fantasy

I've had where we're both engaged in an interesting conversation and when it comes my turn to say something, your mouth actually stops moving." She can be such a smarty pants.

Spot is laying on the floor at the foot of the bed, making funny noises in her sleep. I don't know why, but it sounds as if she's saying "huevos," which means "eggs" in Spanish. Maybe I should slip her one of my allergy pills. That'll straighten her right out — which reminds me, I've got to take my pills before I fall asleep.

A sure sign of middle age is having lots of prescriptions and subscriptions, but elective reading material is another subject altogether. I keep my current prescriptions in a bathroom drawer. I keep old pills in a box with old keys that I also have no idea what they're for, but can't throw out. I've got a few of those empty black and grey plastic film canisters as well. Sometimes I put stray pills in them and sometimes odd keys, but I never, never put both keys and pills in the same one. That just wouldn't be right. Some people store their pills in a special box, to keep them away from little kids. That's a good idea. These days child-proof caps are not enough, especially when kids have such hands-on experience with high explosives.

I think I'll go into the bathroom and put out my pills for later. I take enough pills so that by the time I'm 60 I'll have to rent a room next to a pharmacy. Or buy the pharmacy and put a cot in the back. And speaking of backs — I've got back pain. And neck pain. I have a bad wrist that swells up when the weather changes. Right now, it's getting harder to open a peanut butter jar. Pretty soon, I won't be able to golf, or work out. Sound too good to be true? Wait, there's more!

Last year there was something growing on my leg. I'd never seen anything like it before. Whatever the stuff was, it was really itchy and red and disgusting. And it was creeping up my inner thigh toward my . . . uh, you know.

My doctor said, "I'll take a look. Take off your pants and put on one of those little paper coats in the closet. I'll be back in a moment." As soon as he closed the door, I realized I had a problem.

The doctor was a good friend. We'd played golf together. But he'd never actually given me a full physical. The thought of showing him any part of my groin area made me very uncomfortable. I just couldn't do it. When he came back in I still had my clothes on.

He said, "You know, I could've sworn the last thing I asked you to do was take off your pants and . . ." he reached into the small linen closet and pulled out a paper smock . . . "and put on one of these."

"I know," I said, "but I, uh . . . just can't show you my dick."

"Would it help if I showed you mine, first?" he said.

Before I could say a word, he unbuckled his belt and dropped his pants to the floor. That's when the nurse walked in. She looked at me, looked at him, paused, and said she'd come back. She took two steps toward the door, stopped suddenly, turned around, ripped off her top, and said, "What the hell. I want in. What's the ante?"

*

THE HOOD ORNAMENT IS NOT in the bathroom. But I did get a good idea: If I don't find it I'll just use the bathtub faucet instead. All I have to figure out is how to explain it to Laura when she turns on the tub and a blast of water shoots her in the larynx.

While I'm in here, I might as well take a shower. No — I must take a shower. Phew!

Suddenly I catch my reflection in the mirror. I'm not sure I completely like what I see. Each time I see myself, my hair is a little grayer, my jowls a little lower, the bags beneath my eyes a little fuller. Yet they say men are lucky because age gives us "character." I hope not, because the character staring back at me is beginning to look a lot like Elmer Fudd.

This realization drives some men to want to turn back the clock. For some, this desire can be satisfied by means of a young girlfriend. But eventually going dancing every night until 2 a.m.

leaves a guy clutching his heart. Many men use a less painful process to halt, or at least shape, their aging. Plastic surgery.

"At your age it's really quite easy. Maybe half an hour. A couple cuts, push around in there, and then just suck it out."

"Suck what out?"

"Your fat."

"What do you do with it afterwards?"

"Well, We can recycle it. Maybe you'd like bigger lips. Lots of actresses do it. Do you like Mick Jagger?"

"Can you use it, uh . . . anywhere else?"

"If you're asking me can we inject your fat through a needle right into your penis — sure we can, but it does have a low success rate and there can be side effects. For instance, have you ever seen a penis with jowls? Oh, and this only increases thickness, of course, not length. Does becoming thicker appeal to you?"

"Why yes, I have always dreamed of becoming girthy."

"Okay, so you'll be a bit puffy, swollen — black and blue for about a week, and then the skin will fall back in to place."

"You mean it won't just hang?"

"No. You have great skin tone. But if it hangs then I take a snip here and move it back over there." Piece of cake.

This sounds a lot like my mechanic and I discussing some custom body work at the speed shop, not that I would ever have anything done. I'm the kind of guy who, if he likes something, wears it out. I'm afraid that if I had one part of my face fixed, I'd keep changing more and more. Pretty soon I'd look like a Picasso painting with two eyes on one side of the nose and a complete rearrangement of my face.

However, compared to what women go through to look good, men have it easy. I'm amazed at all the ointments, lotions, conditioners, powders, creams, pencils, and pluckers that women have, and that's not even counting their extensive hair care product line. I'm not saying I don't understand the principle involved. I know first impressions mean a lot, and that a little base and blush can help in any situation. I know this because — as I said earlier — between TV, movies and photo shoots I wear a lot of makeup, more than my wife, actually. Laura has very pretty skin and doesn't need it. Laura *does* have drawers of odd chemical compounds that she probably has to buy on the cosmetic black market. Collagen. Emulsion. Oil of Old Lady. I have no idea what this stuff is. I have to assume it's what she uses to keep her fabulous skin fabulous. All I know is that it really works. I once used one of her products because I grew a zit right before doing a TV interview. This is like having a pimple on prom night. I didn't want to go out in public with it preceding me, particularly since at my age, zits are very distinctive. Laura gave me something to make the zit disappear. It went away in less than two hours. But reappeared in the form of a bad hair day.

Say, how come I didn't know about this stuff in high school?

*

M EN ALSO HAVE an easier time with clothes. I'd be happy anywhere in a short-sleeved shirt and jeans. Not women. Look at how they dress. It's not for us, is it? It's for each other. How do I know? Because all they talk about is what they wear.

"Oh my god, I love your new dress!"

"Do you really? It's just that I have five other black dresses."

"You can never have too many. Besides, your A-line one is raw silk, and your black halter's hemline is at least a half inch shorter. The rhinestone strapless screams 'I'll have another martini please,' and your Donna Karan dress is a *black classic* that can easily take you to a funeral where you're definitely going to weep and be taken seriously. With this new Yves Saint Laurent flowing chiffon thing happening, you can go to a funeral, and most likely leave with a date. You've just gotta keep it!"

Men don't talk about clothes. And if we did, it wouldn't be nice since we're by nature competitive.

"Hey Bob, nice trousers. Are those wool?"

"Yeah, well, a wool blend."

"Oooh. That's too bad. These babies are pure wool — only way to go for this guy."

"Yeah? Well I see pleats are back in style, or are your slacks just a little too snug? A man with my height can easily get away with 'snug'— Pure wool, OR wool blend."

"Don't you have to be somewhere?"

Typically men talk about their gadgets. Recently a guy I know wanted to show me his new Motorola cell phone. "No bigger than a pack of cigarettes," he said. "Cost two grand." He was actually proud of this. Then he showed me his new Hi-8 Handycam. "Two grand." Then new golf clubs with heads made of some newly discovered, highly unstable element, with a half-life of 72 holes or one weekend of tournament play. "Two grand," he said, again.

Did I mention that he wore a t-shirt with holes and old boxer shorts that looked like he hadn't changed them in a week? Ends up — Two grand. I think he was living in his car.

Because women care so much about how they present themselves, they read magazines like *Cosmopolitan* and *Vogue* and *Glamour* for advice. Since it's the Nineties, these magazines all have the same editorial message for the new woman: "Just be yourself and like yourself for who you are." That must be why the rest of the magazine is filled with page after page of gorgeous models, very few of whom look anything like the typical reader, who has to sit there staring enviously at the pictures while reluctantly muttering under her breath, "I'm okay. I like me for who *I* am. I don't mind my wide hips because they're a part of me and that's okay. That's fucking okay!"

These models wear clothes no normal woman can wear, and live in a way most women can only dream about. However, the readers and the models do have one surprising thing in common: Despite all looks being the result of a genetic accident that turns one woman into a lumpish housefrau and another into someone who can rake in millions simply staring vacantly at a camera, neither seem to be very happy with their appearance.

Who says God doesn't have a sense of humor?

*

R IGHT NOW I'M WEARING no pants and no shirt because I'm still waiting for the shower water to get warm. I keep promising myself to install a hot water circulating pump, but I haven't gotten around to it. Let me be more specific: I haven't gotten around to calling the plumber yet to tell him to do it. Actually, I haven't gotten around to looking up his number because I lost the Yellow Pages. So every time I want to take a shower, I have to stand around in the bathroom for five minutes waiting for the climate to change. Come to think of it, what happened to the plumber and the tile man today? I can't get away with just deciding not to show up for work!

This transition from cold to hot, for some reason reminds me of how relationships form and romance works between the sexes. We have a couple minutes to discuss this while the water heats up.

Of course, in love, Heisenberg's Uncertainty Principle applies. Love is a quantum process.

Before a couple meets, they don't exist for each other. They are like two atoms of different elements hoping for a random collision that will lead to the formation of a molecule and eternal togetherness. Atoms of the same element can also join together, but the result is not a new molecule, just more of the same old thing, and they choose to live in special neighborhoods and have parades once a year.

A good way to picture love as this process is to consider salt. Yes, good ol' salt. Sodium chloride, the best thing on a fresh summer beefsteak tomato. Salt is composed of a sodium (Na) and chlorine (Cl). For you technical folks, that's Na2 and Cl2, the molecular forms of both elements. According to chemists, these elements meet during what's called their "free radical" form. I call it the late high school/early college years. Think of these love birds, Na+ and Cl- in their "free radical" state, as latent with passion, about to get horny, and ready to consummate.

That's all very nice, but the real question is why do sodium and chloride even get together and end up on your dinner table? Scientists say that even with the billions of Na+'s and Cl-'s buzzing around in a frenzy, the reaction time needed between the two to form NaCl is much too quick to fit within the mathematical odds of interaction. It's almost as if it's not supposed to happen — and it doesn't always, since there's plenty of each element around on its own.

Yet we have salt, so something else must be going on. Quantum physicists figure that this "something else" is related to the idea of everything having both a wave nature and a particle nature.

First, picture the Na+ and Cl- atoms as the tiny, hard, elemental particles that actually join together. So what is the wave component? Advanced physicists describe the elements' wave natures as "informational fields." In other words, these fields are a kind of instruction set that tell the particles what they're supposed to do. Apparently these included instructions that *alter the odds of pure chance and mutual attraction*. Put yet another way, some information in the wave nature of both sodium and chloride suggest that under certain conditions they're *supposed to be together*. It's as if each knew instinctively that the other "liked" them and maybe they could get lucky. When they meet this feeling clicks in and somehow helps overcome the initial shyness and enormous odds against random interaction.

Now extend this idea to human interaction and the odds against finding the right mate. You meet someone by chance but somehow feel an instant connection, as if you were meant to be together. This feeling that apparently comes out of nowhere — a sense that you know intuitively is not simply the result of a first impression, or looks, smell, charming laughter, great figure, wonderful smile, and all the rest — keeps you talking and interacting just long enough for all the other factors to take hold. And when it's right, it's really right.

Now we have an honest-to-goodness quantum physics explanation for what we commonly call "chemistry" or soul mates, kismet, or fate. And the more you go into this idea, the more it applies. Love isn't as common as they tell us in books and movies and song. It takes something extra to first find the right person and then to see it through. That something "beyond explanation" may well be contained in our personal wave nature's "informational field."

And to think that until now all we had to go on were horoscopes, pheremones, and dating services.

Once the free radical forms Na+ and Cl- unite, the joining is nothing short of exhilarating — from an atomic point of view. The friction and heat and energy produced by the initial merging can last for milliseconds, or about four years in human terms. And then Na+ and Cl- evolve into a stable married couple; salts of the earth, if you will.

Alas, sometimes boredom sets in and, longing for their free radical days, a kinky sodium atom might suggest doing it with or watching two chlorine atoms do it. Given these elements' personalities, it's not so far-fetched. Na2 (sodium) is a bright, volatile metal that explodes into flame when it comes into contact with moisture. Think of him as a young Italian stud. Elemental chlorine is a pretty green gas that causes the eyes to tear, drains the color from anything it touches, and is highly poisonous. Just ask anyone who's fought on the battlefields of World War One. In fact, chlorine was one of the first poison gases used in warfare. This is why any sodium atom worth his salt knows that suggesting a menage a trois with two chlorine atoms is a death sentence. This is also why the stuff in your salt shaker doesn't turn green, pour out in a cloud, and kill everyone at the table.

However, like human relationships, not all chemical combinations are ultimately stable or long-lasting. Phosphorous and sulfur can easily live next door to each other, but the slightest friction between the two produces a flame and near-instant termination. In other words, it's just like striking a match . . . well actually *it is* a match. Hydrogen and sulfur form hydrogen sulfide, which, while it doesn't blow up and can last a long time, also smells very much like rotten eggs.

Sounds like some marriages we all know. This probably explains why so many books are written to try and help couples who can't get along, can't communicate, and don't feel comfortable in their relationships, help themselves. I try to read them all, usually in the bathroom, even though there's a limit to what you can absorb in only ten minutes. I respect the need for balance. If you let something out, you should take something in, even if it's knowledge.

Here's what I find most fascinating: I tend to agree more with the women's point of view than the men's.

So sue me.

I know other men who feel the same. I went to a party once where more of the men than women had read *Men Are From Mars, Women Are From Venus*. And both of them said the same thing I did: "Really cleared up a lot."

These books *are* liberating. Most guys don't want to know what you feel. It's none of their business, and they like it that way. They don't want you to feel bad, but that's about it. Normally, a guy couldn't call another guy and say, "You ever felt like this?"

But now it's: "Ever feel like this?"

"Yeah."

"How about like that?"

"A little of this, a little of that. What's your point?"

Okay, we're still new at it, and pretty soon the talk will turn to cars, computers, and sports.

This new viewpoint even shows up in my relationship with my wife.

For example, Laura and I will often have this little exchange:

ME: "You've got to tell me how you feel."
LAURA: "I don't feel like it."

Just like a man, she finds it difficult to talk about what's bothering her. I see things more like a woman: If she won't tell me what's bothering her, I assume it has something to do with *me.* So I try to get her to express her feelings more than she tries to get me to reveal mine, which means that in our marriage sometimes *she's* the man and I'm the woman. Now you know why I like belted gowns in the summertime and she likes cowboy boots in bed. And when it comes to bed, then, because I *am* the man, — *I'm* definitely the man and she's the woman. I mean, there's only so far you can push Mother Nature, whether you're sleeping on a queen-size bed or not.

*

M Y SHOWER WATER finally got hot and the experience was nothing short of cleansing. I know you're sorry you missed it, but just because you get to look inside my mind doesn't mean you get to leer at my nakedness, too. Anyway, now I feel great. After I brush my teeth and take my pills I can start looking for the hood ornament in the bedroom.

Yech! This bathroom cup doesn't look right. There's some sort of white crust along the edge and I'm not about to drink out of it. This wouldn't be a problem except that I've already got one pill disintegrating in my mouth, spreading its acidic, metallic flavor, and two more in my hand. I need to get a new cup in the kitchen. Might as well get the dog's pills while I'm there. I just have to remember which is which.

Got the cup, got Spot's pills in my left hand. No, mine. No, Spot's. Mine. Ahh, I'll just take a shot and shove these little blue ones down Spot's throat and hope I'm not giving her a dose of Clariton-D. On the other hand, she might thank me in the morning because her sinuses will be so clear that she'll suddenly be able to smell next week.

*

THE ANSWERING MACHINE LIGHT is blinking. Someone must have called while I was in the shower. Isn't that always the way it goes? Five blinks, five calls. I was only in the shower for ten minutes. Does everyone get together beforehand and decide to call all at once?

Beep. "Tim, this is Ron. I can't find anything here that might work as a temporary hood ornament. Sorry. Guess I won't drop by. You'll have to get into trouble on your own tonight. See ya later."

Great. I wonder how long it will take to pull the bathtub faucet?

Beep. "Click."

A hang up. Cowards! I hate hang ups. It's not fair. If someone called me by mistake, I want to know who they were trying to reach and what they wanted. I don't mind wrong numbers so much if they're entertaining, like a call from Ed McMahon:

"Angel Mercado! You are our new $10 million Publisher's Clearing House winner. To claim your prize you must call us at 1-800-555-1111 within thirty minutes."

Sorry, Angel doesn't live here.

Beep. "Honey, it's me. I couldn't get the cell phone to work but I found a pay phone at the Ranger station, so I thought I'd give you a try. And Kady wanted to say goodnight."

"Goodnight, Daddy."

"Hope everything is okay. Kady and I are having a great time. You're probably hanging out with Ron, having a blast. We love you. We miss you. See you tomorrow. Bye."

Great. Not a call I wanted to miss.

Beep. "Click."

Another hang up. That's unusual. We rarely get them since the number is unlisted. Well, I think some kids have it because occasionally I get pizzas I didn't order, but that's about it.

Beep. "Toolman: Right now I feel like having a great big omelette. You've got the eggs."

*

T HAT'S IT! What's going on? This must be some elaborate practical joke. If only I could recognize that voice — but it didn't sound like anyone I know — sort of mechanical, actually — and I replayed it five times. At first, I thought maybe my managers were pulling a fast one, but they couldn't even remember to put my name up for an Emmy, so how could they handle something like this?

I want some answers now. But TAO/MAN says I already have the answers. Everyone says I have the answers.

Tell you what: I think the answer is to get under those covers and forget about it.

*

T HAT LASTED about three minutes. Maybe the ornament is under the bed? I'll just take a look and — whoa, whoa, whoa. What's in *this* box? It's really heavy. Oh. It's ammunition for the shotgun I bought to protect the family. I didn't want to buy a handgun, because that's how people get killed. The shotgun seemed like a better idea, but now I'm thinking it was a boneheaded move. Can you imagine someone breaking into the house in the middle of the night, and me having enough time to get up, get the shotgun out of the bag under the bed — *way* under the bed, and sealed with a combination lock — unlock it, and then load it with ammunition from another locked box, in the pitch black while my heart rate's skyrocketing? I tried it one night as a drill. It took me only 15 minutes to find the boxes in the dark.

I wish Laura was here to help me look. Laura loses stuff much more than I do. She's lost her diamond wedding ring three times. Once, my dad found it in the front yard. He was mowing the lawn and saw something glitter.

The first time Laura lost her ring she didn't even tell me. If she had just said, "Gee, I lost my ring," I wouldn't have thought two ways about it. But since she withheld information that made it significant, I thought, "Well, it is *her* diamond ring. And it's *our* marriage." Pretty soon I was lost in unhealthy symbolism.

I had the same suspicions the time Laura bought me an antique aviator's watch for Christmas. I have a thing for antique timepieces, but she must know me better than I realize because although I never actually told her about this particular watch, or pointed it out in any way, there it was on Christmas morning. To this day she won't tell me how she knew. The only thing I can come up with is that I talk in my sleep. Or that she's learned to interpret my snores.

Or perhaps a Tim from a parallel universe told her. I don't know if that counts as cheating, but I'd better not catch them together.

*

I HAD A FANTASY recently and imagined what it would be to get together — overnight — with Martha Stewart.

I don't imagine any lovemaking, but rather the morning after. Every time I think about it I get really excited because Martha is just on fire with creativity. I really admire her.

Here's what happens: I open my eyes and first notice that my clothes from the night before are neatly folded in a pyramid shaped stack with a decorative string of dried pea pods painted gold, binding them together. There's Martha, already dressed in a crew-neck sweater and pleated slacks, perfectly coifed, looking just like she looks on TV.

"Good morning," I say. "You're up early."

"Yeah. I made you a newspaper. That's all rice paper, you know. And that's balsamic vinaigrette. You can eat it like a scone once you're done reading it."

"You made the newspaper?"

"Yeah. I just finished the press last week. I made a newspaper press out of tweed and some cotton fiber."

"You made a newspaper press? That's interesting."

"Thanks. And I gathered all the news myself using a complex system of charming carrier pigeons who live in the barn loft."

"Really!"

"All the glass in this house I blow myself. I have a smelter out in the hand-hewn woodshed."

"You make . . . ?"

"Yeah, I've also got a bauxite mine in Idaho that we dug out. Because I can my own organic garden vegetables, I thought it would be better if I made my own cans. Then I could get good quality."

"Martha, I notice that while we're talking you're stepping in grapes."

"Yes, I'm making my own wine."

"Your lingerie last night was very sexy."

"Made that. Raised the silkworms. I also grow cotton for my everyday skivvies. You see the cotton out there?" She points out the window.

"You spin your own cotton?"

"Yes."

"Listen, do you mind if I call my wife? I don't want her to get suspicious."

"Fine. Let me get you the phone I built from civil war kitchen utensils I collected from swap meets in the South."

"You built the phone?"

"Yes. And that camcorder over on the table which we will use to document the bird feeder we're going to build together out of that scented spruce tree in the back."

Of course, this would never happen. I've already met Martha and we got along fine. She even lets me fool around in her workshop now and then — as long as I don't touch anything.

*

THE BEDROOM IS the spiritual home to both Laura and me, of our marriage. It's where we make love and make plans. It is where we've made our own private history. Not too long ago we both came across a picture of ourselves taken at someone's wedding nearly 20 years before. We both immediately laughed and said, "Geez, where did that 20 years go?"

As the years have passed, our relationship has become more mature and more dangerous at the same time. The things about each of us that make our marriage so strong are also those things than can cause the most turmoil. They are two sides of the same coin. Once again, it's the quantum nature of love.

After all this time, I didn't expect so much understanding from Laura. It takes a lot of that on both sides. We've had periods where one or both of us hasn't been healthy, or nice, and the other person's dealt with it and helped make it better. She's been through job changes. I've been through this celebrity thing that's changed me, her, the family, and just about everything else. Had we stayed in Michigan and had none of this life happened, I have no idea what we would have done. I might not have even stayed in comedy. The road work would have eventually dried up and the money wouldn't have gone as far. I probably would have tried to get into local TV with a cheesy talk/variety show.

"Today, a little bit of Venus and Mars in the bedroom, right here on Earth. A Wisconsin cheese farmer from over in Mantiwoc, who claims he was abducted and forced to take an alien bride, has written a book about how to get along with gals who are out of this world."

The most profound truth I've realized after being with the same woman for almost 20 years is that the good seems to be getting better, and the bad seems to be getting less bad. I love looking at her more. I love being around her more. I trust her more.

If it only wasn't so one-sided, it might work out.

*

AS I LIE HERE in bed, it just overwhelms me when I think about how much I love Laura. Of course in our society, the word "love" is misused. People say, "I love pizza." "I love bowling." "I love my Toyota." But what they really mean is "I really enjoy the sensory feedback, or pleasure, that these things bring me."

If desperate, I'll sleep with my car or a pizza, but I draw the line at a bowling ball.

During my late night reading I've discovered that the human brain has a region called the limbic, or "lower" brain, and it is the physical origin of lust, fear, anger, and all physical pleasure. Think of it as sort of the "Tijuana" of the brain. This fun area works in a knee-jerk reaction way with hardly any input from the cerebral cortex, or "higher" brain, where love, compassion, courage, happiness, forgiveness, and complex reasoning reside. Of course, these areas aren't actually separate, but totally integrated and interactive. When I page through the Victoria's Secret catalog or swimsuit issue of *Sports Illustrated*, my lower brain just wants to start chewing the magazines. Even if my face and body language don't show it, a small part of me is acting like that horny wolf in the cartoons, who howls and smashes his head on the table while steam shoots from his ears. Fortunately, my trusty higher brain remembers that I'm very happily married to an exquisite woman whom I love deeply, and who is also a crack shot. By the way, all of this happens quicker than my sweaty hand can turn a page.

The brain's limbic region is common to all mammals, but unlike other animals, the *human* brain has that huge cerebral cortex, which means we're usually a lot cooler and a lot more in control than the rest of the animal kingdom, except at hockey games and stag parties.

Love is a function of the higher brain, which means love is not just sexual pleasure, although that certainly seems to be part of it, especially when Laura and I make up after a fight. The love I feel for Laura is continuous. Even when we're really pissed off at each other, there's this ever-present, although momentarily forgotten, love thing.

I read somewhere that nine out of ten Americans think that love is essential to their personal happiness, but I'm willing to bet that every one of them has a different definition of love. The song-writer Victor Herbert says it's the "sweet mystery of life." But Dean Martin says it's "whena the moon hitsa you eye like a bigga pizza pie." Maybe they're both saying the same thing. In fact, since the beginning of time, people have tried to define the essence and experience of love in books, songs, paintings, greeting cards, and tattoos they got when they were drunk. Love is a human preoccupation second to . . . no, second to nothing. It's what we do.

When I was a philosophy major in college, I read that Plato said something like: "Loving someone is our way of appreciating the essence of beauty and goodness within that person." So, in some way our observation seems to participate in creating the beauty that we love. Remember that the physicists say that we participate in creating the world we *observe* by the act of observing. Hmmm. Plato uses the word "essence" and the dictionary definition of "essence" is: a basic underlying or constituting entity, substance, or form. As far as the "goodness" in Plato's definition, well, in Confucianism there is a basic principle called "Jen," which is the belief that there is pure "goodness" at the center of our being, which is a reflection of the goodness at the center of everything — and that's God. Hmmm. So love is God and God is love. It's no wonder I feel overwhelmed by my love for Laura and no wonder it's continuous, since its origin is God.

I think I see the first lightening flashes of a major brainstorm.

Remember when I said a lot of physicists see the universe as a seamless undivided wholeness and that it's been definitely proven that reality is "non-local," which means that we're all connected to everything and to everybody? Well, the mystics and now the physicists seem to agree that our separateness from the world and each other is an illusion of the five senses.

Our sense of ourselves as separate and totally physical, as defined by our five senses, is called ego. The ego is loaded with fear, since it feels isolated and knows it has a limited shelf-life, so to speak.

However, I believe there is also a part of ourselves that is aware of our connectedness and not limited to the five senses and the physical body. Call it our spirit or soul or whatever. When that part of ourselves touches that same part in another person, love is the result.

The romantic and sexual fireworks, while fun and sometimes dangerous, as fireworks often are, just light up the way to this deeper love. Of course, sometimes the fireworks are so exciting that they're mistaken for the real thing and a relationship never deepens. When two people make love and experience an orgasm so intense that it makes the neighbor's cable go out, it can get confusing. But as the Zen saying goes, "You may use the finger to point at the moon, but once you see the moon, the finger is no longer essential."

Or as my Italian friend from New York says, "Don't get hung up on the flash and the bang."

Trust comes automatically with real love because this deep connectedness wipes out ego's isolation and fear. It says this right on the dollar bill: "In God We Trust." They didn't say, "In Love We Trust," because our founding fathers thought it might be a psychological disadvantage when our country went to war. As I said earlier, people think hate is the opposite of love. It's not. Love and hate are closely related. Crimes of passion come to mind:

HOMICIDE DETECTIVE: "Why did you shoot your husband thirty
    times, Mrs. Rodriguez?"
MRS. RODRIGUEZ: "Because I loved him so much . . . and I ran
    out of ammo . . . and the stores were closed."

Fear — the opposite of love — comes from a feeling of separateness and impermanence. Laura and I are never really afraid of each other because in a fundamental way we know we are one.

Now I've probably pissed off some of the lunatic fringe of the radical feminists, and since I don't want a Molotov Tampon thrown at my car, I'll explain. While we both acknowledge that we are separate, fully empowered, and unique individuals on one level, on another level we share "Unity Consciousness" and our love has its source in God, the source of all things. We are instinctively in touch with God through our love and this also goes a long way toward eliminating the other element of fear, which is impermanence, since God has an eternal shelf life and is also the shelf.

You know what? I miss my wife.

*

I'M LONELY. Yes, I wanted a weekend by myself, but I didn't mean that I wanted to sleep here without Laura. I don't like being alone in the bedroom with no one else in the house. Ever since I was a kid it meant weird things would happen.

I remember once, when I was little, I was watching the *Sheriff Scotty Show*. At one point he turned to the screen and said, "And that goes for everybody." Then he looked right at *me* and said, "That also means you down there sucking on your little finger."

I was doing exactly that. How could Sheriff Scotty know that? Sure, if he'd said thumb, that could have been a thousand kids, but no, he said little finger. He blew my seven-year-old mind. Freaked me right out. I ran downstairs and tried to tell my mom. She said it didn't happen. Of course it happened. It *did* happen. He looked down right at me!

I think I'll play it safe and watch my movie.

*

I GOT MYSELF a snack of low-sodium, low-fat Triscuits. If they were lower in anything else the box would be empty. I really like them, though, because that's all I could find in the cabinet. I've also got a little cognac and some cheese.

Forbidden Planet is my favorite film. There are two parts I especially like, one frightening and one wonderful. The first is when the Id, or the monster from Morpheus, makes its shape seen in the ray-gun blasts. It's this horrible head with legs. A great monster. If you're a child it leaves so much to your imagination. The second, wonderful, part is the absolutely stunning, cheesy effect of seeing the vast Krell city underground. The whole inside of the planet is a machine. It can generate as much power as these modern physics guys talk about us having in the next millennium when we will supposedly be able to harness the energy of the sun.

One reason I like this movie is because it takes you from everything being bad to having hope.

Wait. I don't believe it.

No, it's not possible . . . in the background, on the wall of the Krell city, I thought I just saw the hood ornament. Come on. It can't be. I know — I'll just back up the laser disc a few frames and look again. Jeez . . . Why can't I ever get this player remote to work when I want it to? Alright. There we go. There's the alien . . . a couple more seconds . . . There it is again! Freeze frame! The wall switch lever: *it's the hood ornament*! This is bullshit! How can that be? That's not possible. Maybe it just looks that way because I'm 20 feet away. Okay, now I'm standing right next to the TV monitor. Yes, it's the hood ornament.

I don't believe this.

I don't think I can watch this movie any more.

*

TAO/MAN — whoever he is — is right: Nothing is as it seems. I'm frightened. Obviously I've got to rethink everything that's happened to me today. For a while it seemed like fun, then curiously interesting, but now it's scary. There's no way anyone could have put the image of the hood ornament on the disc of *Forbidden Planet*. I know it was never there before.

And why the hood ornament? Why should something I've been looking for all day show up on a laser disc? I mean, if I'd seen a People's Choice award in the movie, I would have been concerned, but this is personal. Is there more to the ornament than I suspected?

I think it may be the key to everything. Or at least the key to my sanity. Or insanity. I can't decide — and it's driving me nuts.

But if it *is* an answer, or God forbid, *the* answer, then why did those homeless guys say I *already* had the answer? I don't know what to think. All I know is that this thing is more than a mere hunk of metal and glass. But I *already* knew that on the day I bought it.

I've got to keep focused. I don't want to go over the edge. And here's a thought: It's only been since I got the ornament that I started reading all these science and philosophy books in earnest, and losing more and more sleep. Maybe touching the ornament was the first catalyst and unbeknownst to me, I've been preparing myself since then for the day I'd touch it again.

I'll keep looking for the ornament in the morning. But I realize I also have to think more about these "answers" that I now know are intimately bound up with my midlife malaise, detachment, and curiosity about the nature of reality and existence. I have to look *now* for the answers, and trust that the hood ornament will be found when it's ready to be found.

It's almost midnight. I need to rest. I am mentally exhausted. TAO/MAN said I should to look into my dreams. It's too late to stop now.

*

I'm in a building the size of a convention center. The walls are made of tuck 'n roll padding in muted silver gray. The ceiling is studded with little gymnasium lights. The building is divided lengthwise down the middle. The long center wall goes from ceiling to floor. There are two openings in the wall, near either end, so you can get from side to side. Smaller walls jut out about six feet from the side walls at two points, dividing each side wall into thirds.

The whole thing is filled halfway with water. It seems about thirty feet deep.

I'm in the water, treading furiously, and I'm being chased by four men in a motorboat. No matter where I try to hide, they find me. They're screaming something at me, chasing me. Sometimes when they get close, I dive deep, and let them race by above me. I'm trying desperately to get away. I have to keep swimming around the middle wall because if I get stuck in a corner I'm finished.

I've managed to keep away from them for what seems like hours, but finally, I can't take it any more. I see the boat hurtling toward me, hear the men screaming, and decide to hell with it. I swim away from the wall and out into the open and tread water in the boat's path. They race closer. The water suddenly gets colder. The boat slows and stops right next to me. One man raises his arms. I close my eyes.

"Kill me," I say. "Just kill me and get it over with."

Then I hear someone shout: "What's the matter with you? Get in the damn boat. Didn't you hear us yelling at you? We've been trying to rescue you. Get in the damn boat!"

*

MY EYES SNAP OPEN and I wake up in the dark.

What? It's only 12:09 a.m.? I've been asleep for less than 15 minutes. I can't go through this again.

And that dream. I had it when I was a kid, many times. But that was long ago. And now, suddenly, it's back. Only this time it was different. Very different.

I'm not going to think about any of this until the morning.

SUNDAY

NINE

IT'S . . . 8:45 A.M. The day
fiters through the blinds into my bedroom, throwing lines of sun
and shadow on everything. They remind me of my life: light and
dark, good and bad, clarity and confusion. I see all the parts, and
have no sense of wholeness. But step back and it all becomes light
through a window. I think that may be what I'm searching for even
if I don't always realize it.

The dream I had last night I've had before. The first time it
came I was just a kid. My father was still alive. Each time I'd try
desperately to keep away from the speedboat until my lungs were
ready to burst. Each time I'd wake up exhausted and drenched in
sweat, and wondering why.

It wasn't my first recurring dream, either. Once, when I had a
high fever, I dreamed someone sawed the Earth in half and threw
one half on top of me. Talk about responsibility, not to mention
strength. Where's Atlas when you need him? Another time I dreamt
that my brothers and family suddenly got deep empty eye sockets

and moved quickly toward me and I couldn't get away. On second thought, I'd call that one a nightmare. Compared to both, the boat dream was a relief, but that's like saying the frying pan is better than the fire. You still burn, it just takes longer and you're a bit more flavorful.

Last night the boat dream was different. It was the *first time* I stopped trying to escape. I'd like to say it was because something in me just had to confront my pursuers and demand and explanation, but the truth is, I was just weary and ready to give up. I surrendered totally to my fate. If I was guilty of something, or innocent, it didn't matter. I'd had enough. So to hear the guy say, "We've been trying to save you. Get in the damn boat," completely blew my mind. It was the last thing I expected.

It makes me realize how much our own expectations narrow our vision.

The message was loud and clear: Face your fears.

Surviving my dream is one reason I feel pretty good today. I've been awake for five minutes and my mood is still upbeat. That impresses even me.

*

THE PETS ARE FED, the house alarm is off, and now I'm ready for the Sunday paper. It's usually at the far end of the driveway, which means I can take Spot for a very short walk.

I've developed a whole organizing routine for the paper. I'm so into the details that it's the only truly Buddhist thing I do. I think I have more fun shuffling the sections for my ceremonious preparation than actually reading them. First, I lift and separate. Then, and I'm sure the LA *Times* advertising department doesn't want to hear this, I immediately take out all their ads, personals, and classifieds.

I start by reading the front page. Lately, though, it seems like wasted space because I've seen it all on TV the night before, or on CNN or Headline News. The newspaper can go more into depth than the common sound bite, but who has the time? If *I* did, I wouldn't eat at McDonald's. Also, the "news" is generally bad and depressing, and who wants to dwell on those details? I get enough of that with the local TV news.

"Prison break horrifies local community! Film at 11." They give no clue in which local community the cons are running loose. And why? So you'll stay tuned for the info, of course. Now, what if the escapees are in *your* neighborhood and they break into *your* house and kill *you* before 11 p.m.? That's why whenever a jail break happens I think I really oughta know all the specifics as soon as possible!

Next, I read Travel, Sports, and the Funnies. Also the Real Estate section. I'm not buying or selling, but I can't live without checking the Hot Properties column to see which celebrity is buying what, where. So if Ricardo Montalban shows up at my front doorstep to borrow a cup of sugar, I'll know to wear my house robe made of rich, Corinthian leather.

Then I read the Entertainment section and try to figure out who these people are who get quoted in the full page movie ads. Take a look at the quotes: "Funniest this summer." "I cried till I laughed!" (. . . and this was *Schindler's List*). And who the heck are the *Radioland News*, *QRS Network*, *Sixty Second Preview*, and the *New York Times*? Is there no watchdog to police this stuff? There's no law against lying or taking quotes out of context. You could actually say: "'Spectacular!' John Vomit, Senile News Service." The real review probably said, "The movie falls *way short* of spectacular."

What really holds my interest are science stories. I'd much rather learn about mankind's expeditions along the scientific frontier than yet again read about racism, sexism, and other negative "isms." When I'm so thrilled about new discoveries and ways of thinking about existence, it really steams me to see those stories side-by-side with others about church burnings, human brutality, divisive politics, and crass self-aggrandizement.

One recent example comes to mind:

Scientists are soon expecting verification of life on Mars. This would imply that we are living in a universe teaming with life, including, most probably, other intelligent life. Yet, on the front page it was also revealed that many leading senators were helping the tobacco companies open up the Chinese market. When asked to comment on the fact that this could cause potentially 300 million deaths, one senator commented, "It's our contribution in containing the overpopulation explosion." Wait a minute. Wasn't that one of Hitler's excuses?

What the hell's the matter with us? Why do we persist in making believe that we're not part of each other and the earth we live on? We really need to grasp this idea of being connected if we're going to evolve, much less survive. Yet we see the world as fragmented, as parts warring against other parts. I know this has a lot to do with our sensory apparatus and the Western, reductionist (breaking into elemental parts) nature of science and religion, but the idea of unity is nothing new. In fact it's been around a long time. It's time we gave it a serious try.

I'd even settle for a semi-serious try. Okay, how about starting small with the goal being unity in the family?

I don't mean to preach. This is just what I go through every Sunday morning. Besides, it's been a long time since I've been in the house of God, although I've been to the House of Pancakes and to the House of Blues. Had a great time in both places. Why don't they start a place called The House of Blue Pancakes? Would that count? Sometimes I think we should join a church for Kady's sake. We've raised her with a strong moral background and a more formal religious and spiritual education could only enhance that, as long as Laura and I are around to do our part at home. I might even find a few answers for myself in church, as well.

Not that I have the time, you understand.

Before I do anything I have to eat. Since I'm alone, I'll have scrambled eggs my way: a little runny, a little bit of cheese, loaded with hot sauce and salsa. And some toast. Usually I eat them straight from the pan, but this time I'll use a plate because the blister on my tongue still hasn't healed from the last time.

*

THERE'S THE PHONE. I hope it's Laura and Kady. Or the plumber, with a great excuse.

"Hullo."

"Tim. It's Matthew Newman."

Wow. A voice from the past. Matthew is an actor. I haven't seen him for a while. The last time we hung out he had a pretty serious drinking problem. In fact, he managed to drink away a hit TV show and a six-figure salary. Then, I heard he went to a clinic to get rehabilitated.

"How are you, Matthew? Long time." I wonder why he's calling.

"I'm great. Really great."

"Good. So, are you . . . "

"Yes. I'm in the program now. Almost two years."

"AAA?"

"No, AA. AAA is the Automobile Club of America."

Shit, I knew when I said it, it was wrong.

"I guess this means I have to call you Matt D. now."

"Only at meetings."

"So, what are you working on?"

"I just got back from South America."

"You're kidding."

"No, I went to Venezuela."

"Seems to be on a lot of people's minds."

"Guess so. I did a *National Geographic* TV special about these incredible rock formations that are billions of years . . . "

"Tepuis?"

"Yeah. You've been?"

"No. But I've . . . read about them."

"Something wrong, Tim?"

"No. It's just . . . been a crazy weekend. That sounds fascinating. So what's going on? Why . . . "

"Well, Tim, to tell you the truth, I just joined a church near you and I remembered that the last time we hung out you said you wanted to go, but could never find the time."

"I said that?"

"Yes. You also said you didn't go because you were afraid that because you're on TV you might disrupt things."

"Right. I remember."

"Well, I belong to this small church near you, and they've got other show biz people in the congregation. So I'm basically taking a shot in the dark and calling to see if maybe you and the family want to join me for the service today."

"My wife and daughter are on a camping trip."

"Well, how about you?"

How about me?

This is clearly synchronicity. In fact, if I remember my reading correctly, this is what the first couple chapters of the *Celestine Prophecy* is about. The book is one man's supposedly true story of a journey to Peru in pursuit of nine ancient Insights that will help mankind evolve, but the Peruvian government and church are trying to suppress them. I didn't really buy all that baloney about hacking through the jungle and the crazy monks, but the message *is* important.

The first insight said that we're all looking for more meaning in life. It suggested that we pay closer attention to what seem like coincidences in our lives because — I knew I was on to something — they are actually examples of synchronicity. If we keep our eyes open and follow them we will start on the road to spiritual truth.

That hits my nail right on my head, doesn't it? Might as well go with the river in the direction it's flowing.

"I haven't been to church since we spoke," I tell Matthew. "But yes, I would like to go. Should I meet you there, or do you want to swing by?"

"It's the Episcopalian Church, about a mile from your house, right next to the Kentucky Fried Chicken."

"I know the one. Maybe you should come get me. You know how you can get fooled in California. The architecture is so erratic and sometimes what looks like a church on the outside . . . "

"Is often a studio head's home?"

"Funny. It's just that the last time I walked into something that was *supposed* to be a church, for a wedding in San Diego, it was really some new age retreat that used to be a church. I think it was the Shrine of the Holy Crystal. Lots of overly happy people welcomed me, in fact they kept hugging me. A small donation finally freed me from their embraces. I don't consider myself a New Age type of guy. I hate the smell of incense, and to me, a near death experience is almost spilling a drink on John Gotti."

"Did you make it to the wedding?"

"Yeah. It was actually a double-wedding. Turns out I *was* in the right place. My friends had both recently become channelers and when their entities met — one was a party girl who became queen of Atlantis, the other was former Russian Premier Leonid Brezhnev — they also fell in love and decided to get hitched."

"That must have been wonderful."

"Yeah. Our friends are doing fine, they bought a house, just had a baby. I hear the entities are fighting, though. Something about whether he'll breathe air or water."

"Oh, wow. Look at the time. Tell you what. I've got to clean up. I'll meet you at the church in about 45 minutes."

It will be good to see Matthew. He sounds very healthy and energetic. The program must be helping. I'd like to spend time with him, catch up, I just hope he doesn't try to preach to me. I'm not in the mood for an evangelical Sunday.

You know, what I really need is to find a meeting of QPA — Quantum Physics Anonymous. But how could they even hold meet-ings? If they set a time, the location would change, and vice versa. Even if everyone managed to get into the same room it would be impossible to know who's there — that's *real* anonymity — without colliding with them each time they spoke. It would save on the chair rentals, though.

I'm glad Matthew called. I'm already in a better mood.

*

WHEN I WAS LITTLE, my brothers and I went to Sunday school while my parents went to church. Back then we always thought attending the service with the adults would be more exciting than our religious lessons. But when my dad finally let us sit in the chapel, it wasn't. Stand up, sing. Sit down, sing. Stand up, sing. Kneel, pray. Get up, pray. Fidget. Listen to a sermon . . . Fidget. Drift off from the sermon. Wake-up and put money in a basket. *My* lawn-mowing money in to a basket? Sunday school suddenly looked like a dream come true.

Church was supposed to be the place where we found the answers to the big questions. The thing is, not only did they provide the answers, but the questions as well. What I don't remember was any sense of inquiry into the veracity or reality of what was taught. Maybe I was too young to notice. Or maybe established religion is by definition beyond question. I guess "established" means they already have the answers they need; all that's left is to follow instructions. The problem for me was that religion always created more questions than answers. Why, for instance, does God let innocents die? When another school bus full of kids rolls over an embankment and bursts into flame, what could God be thinking? Why isn't it a bus of convicted murderers or tobacco company lawyers?

Times were simpler in Sunday school. We only had to learn the story of Christianity and memorize the Ten Commandments.

I wonder if I still remember them all?

(I'm thinking. Maybe I can do them in order.)

Thou shalt have no other Gods before me. No graven images. Don't take the name of the Lord in Vain. (How am I doing?) Keep the Sabbath. Honor your father and mother. Thou shalt not kill. Thou shalt not commit adultery. (We didn't know what it was, we only knew you had to be a grown up to do it. Typically, we couldn't wait.) Thou shalt not steal. No bearing false witness against the neighbors. Thou shalt not covet thy neighbor's wife. Gee, the first time I mowed the neighbor's lawn his wife paid me and gave me a great big smile, and I suddenly felt like doing their lawn forever for free, but I wasn't sure if that fell under the forbidden rules of the church. At the time, it sounded borderline, but I wasn't going to ask.

In Sunday school one invariably hears a lot of paraphrasing: especially of the last commandment. I think Number 10 was more complicated and included things like coveting the neighbor's house, his male or female servants, his ox, his ass — even then this caused sniggers — or anything else he owned, including the color TV, stereo system, and those highball glasses with the arty nudes painted on them.

"Covet" was a strange word. The teachers avoided any kind of reality-based definition. They explained it by saying we shouldn't *desire* anything that belonged to someone else. When I got older, I learned the real meaning of the Commandment: "Keep your hands off your neighbor's wife." They were very specific and focused right in on the problem. Some sinners might like the ox or the ass, but for most of the populace I don't think they picked "wife" by mistake.

I was a good kid. I honored my parents, didn't lie or steal, and wished everyday was the Sabbath. As for coveting, the neighbor's wife was not my type, and the zoning regulations prevented them from having anything but a dog and two cats.

When I got older and stopped going to church, I didn't think much about any of this until I was a comic on the road who had lots of free time between shows. Now and then I'd pick up a hotel room Bible and explore. What I found one day blew my mind. The Ten

Commandments were only the *big ten*. God actually had quite a laundry list. There were many, many lesser commandments. Actually they were warnings or suggestions. But the penalties were nonetheless severe: death.

You don't want to fool around with Mr. Big.

Here's what I found just a few pages after the Commandments. Either there weren't enough stone tablets to fit these, or the whole pile was just too heavy for Moses to carry down the mountain without getting a hernia.

"Whoever lies carnally with a woman who is betrothed to a man as a concubine and who has not at all been redeemed nor given her freedom, for this there shall be scourging. But they shall not be put to death because she was not free."

Scourging? Is this anything like being loofahed by a team of weight lifters using emery boards?

"The man who lieth with his father's wife has uncovered his father's nakedness. Both of them shall surely be put to death. If a man lies with his daughter-in-law, both of them shall surely be put to death."

I understand the wife thing because that's your mother, but what if it's your mother-in-law and you're both drunk on holiday wine? Does this count as perversity or charity?

"If a man mates with an animal, he shall surely be put to death. And you shall kill the animal too!"

Now stop me if I'm out of line, but is this *really* with the poor animal's consent? I'll bet no one ever found any provocative sheep's clothing laying around, either.

"If a man takes his sister, his father's daughter or his mother's daughter, sees her nakedness and she sees his nakedness, it is a wicked thing and they shall be cut off from the sight of their people. He has uncovered his sister's nakedness. He shall bear his guilt."

The only thing they didn't have a law about was bathing with shrubbery.

Unfortunately this didn't leave much to do on a Saturday night except separate the wheat from the chaff and worry about if you've been petting your dog too much. No wonder television's so damn popular now.

*

EVENTUALLY ALL THIS "learning" led to the Catechism, which was like a religious bar exam for kids. This was not fun because you had to go to Sunday school at night to memorize stuff. During study breaks we'd run across the street and get liquored-up on Sweet-tarts and Lik-A-Maid. When the big day came, we had to appear in front of the bishop. He was what's known in Hollywood as a major player. Meeting him was far more frightening than taking the test, but if you passed, you were confirmed and could take communion, which is the wafer and wine, or body and blood of Christ. Taste-wise, I still preferred having a Pez dissolve on my tongue and washing it down with a Yoohoo.

There *was* some fun to be had at church. My brothers and I were acolytes, or little church servants. Since there's a hierarchy involved, and we were budding men, starting our religious careers at an entry position felt right. It was a very big deal to carry the lead cross in the procession, especially at Easter or Christmas services. For me, being part of the whole thing was the most spiritual component, even though I was not crazy about having to wear the funny little robe or kneel on little cushions. Very often kids would pass out because they had to kneel for so long. They'd just keel over.

Acolytes also helped move books for the priest after he was done reading something on the altar. And we'd help him with the wine. But you didn't want to touch or do the wrong thing.

"Don't put this book over here."

"Stop looking at yourself in the chalice!"

And soon, when the novelty wore off, the job offered much fertile ground to a smartass. When you're done with the wine and the water, you have to pour it into the sink. Actually, the Blessed

Sink. My question was: "When it's stopped up do we have to call Joe's Blessed Plumber Service?" I thought I was pretty funny until my mom told me that the Blessed Sink didn't drain into the sewer system. It went straight down into the ground and let the wine dissipate. Being holy wine it may actually sink so deep into the earth that it becomes acid rain in hell.

The problem with all these rules, outfits to wear, proper ways to carry the cross, and the Blessed Sink mystery, is that eventually most of the kids started questioning everything. It's not that we found the rules intellectually and morally phony. We just wanted our Sundays free. We'd look for any excuse not to go to church.

"I'm certain the Sea Monkeys are going to give birth today. As the responsible owner, I really should be there."

"It's funny, but practicing the piano really does seem to help my grades."

"Gee Mom, I thought I could stay home and hem that new skirt for you."

Eventually our parents no longer demanded that we attend. (And my mother never again had to pay for alterations.)

It will be weird to go back as an adult.

*

I FOUND THE CHURCH easily by spotting the Colonel's spinning bucket. Wonder what's really in that bucket? There's Matthew in the parking lot. Wow, he looks great. Young. Younger.

"I'm glad you called," I say. "I'm nervous. It's been a long time since I've prayed in public."

"I'm nervous, too."

"Why?"

"I need to make an amend to you."

"For what? What did you ever do to me?"

He pulled a twenty-dollar bill from his pocket and handed it to me. "I owe you this. I took it from your wallet one night. I needed something to drink. I'm sorry."

Unbelievable!

"Consider it settled." He smiled. Then I said, "Just curious: How'd you get my wallet? I always carry it in my back pocket."

"You were a little gone yourself, pal."

*

MATTHEW IS RIGHT. There are other people from the business here and no one makes a big deal over me. We take our seats and soon the organ music starts. I already know how the next hour will unfold: Stand up, sing. Sit, sing. Stand up, sing more. Sit, sing. Kneel, pray. Still, I feel good just for having gotten out of the house to come.

But I'm having trouble paying attention, and so my eyes start to wander. What I find would have been surprising yesterday but not today. The Communion cup looks a lot like one I saw in my dream about finding the Answers in the hidden room on the Tepui. The stained glass windows have designs that look like jeweled eggs. Next thing you know I'll see the hood ornament. I'm not going to let anything rattle me. Well, maybe a speedboat full of men racing through the chapel would freak me out a bit.

"What are you thinking?" Matthew whispers. I suppose it's not hard to tell my mind is somewhere else.

"You sound like me on a date in high school."

"Are you okay?"

"Well, I was just thinking about a dream I had a couple nights ago."

"About what?"

"You won't believe it."

"Try me."

"The Tepuis."

"Why wouldn't I believe you?"

"Because in my dream I found the Answers to life."

"That's great."

"And then misplaced them."

"Oh. Well, It was only a dream, Tim. Hey, the sermon's starting."

Matthew turns away to listen, but I'm so lost in thought that I can't concentrate on the content, just the rhythm of the minister's delivery. I let my self sink into the syncopation. I don't resist. Light could pour out of my eyes and mouth, and I wouldn't be surprised.

"Great sermon, huh?" says Matthew.

"What?"

"The sermon."

"It's over?"

"Yeah, I thought you were listening."

"No, I drifted . . . what was it about?"

"Judging people. The Sermon on the Mount. Judge not lest ye be judged. Very inspiring."

I hope Matthew doesn't judge me for not listening, but I know that not being judgmental is tough. I consciously try not to be. One of my biggest lessons from a sermon I *did* hear — in prison — was the idea to simply perform one Christian act each day, which would lead to another and then another. It's like the saying we have now, "Think globally, act locally." So each day I try not to be judgmental. I'm not perfect, but my attitude towards others has gradually become much more compassionate. What I do is make believe that anyone I judge is looking at me, thinking, "Yeah, well I'm God. You just fucked with the wrong guy." If, as I've come to believe, everybody has God within them, then judging someone else is like judging myself and judging the Big Boy. That's why it's such a horrible thing to do.

When I was in jail was the first time I asked God to help me not judge. And then I asked him if he'd make it retroactive to the judge who put me in jail.

*

THEY'RE PASSING AROUND the collection plate, so we have to sit for a few more minutes. Finally the man to my left hands me the dish. Not wanting to give up my lawn-mowing money, I drop Matthew's $20 bill on the pile and pass it over to him — and stop mid-pass. I've just seen something I find hard to believe. I take back the plate and poke through the bills and change until I can see the design in the center.

It's the hood ornament, or awfully darn close.

"You know Tim, traditionally you're suppose to keep passing it," whispers Matthew. "Can't you just see this one in the Tabloids? *Tim Allen Won't Loosen His Grip on Church's Collection Plate! The Toolman and God in a Tug of War. See page five.*"

I shake my head from side to side and hand him the plate.

"I couldn't possibly explain."

"Try." His expression is blank, like a page with no writing, waiting to be filled with my words.

"I'm building a hot rod. All that's left is to put on the hood ornament. I bought one a few years ago, a one-of-a-kind piece. This will sound crazy, but when I picked it up I felt strange and warm and just knew I had to have it. I kept it in the garage while I built the car and now, even though I know where I put it for all these years, I can't find it — and I've done almost nothing this weekend except search for the thing because some people are coming by tomorrow to pick up the hot rod for a car show."

"You'll find it."

"Oh, I've found it. Not it, actually, but . . . "

"What are you talking about?"

I push aside the money on the collection plate, ignoring the impatient stares of other parishioners, and point to the design. "Here. This is exactly what the ornament looks like. Why do you suppose it's on the plate but not in my house? And that's not even the weirdest part. Last night I saw the ornament in an old science fiction movie. I've seen the movie a hundred time. It was never there before or at least I never noticed it."

Matthew takes the plate, puts money on the pile, and passes it on. He doesn't seem surprised at all.

"Well, Tim, an increase in synchronicity in someone's life is said to indicate a transition to a higher stage of enlightenment."

"Synchronicity, shminchronicity. I'm freaking out. All I want is to be enlightened about where the ornament is."

"Deepak Chopra, in *The Way of the Wizard*, says it indicates the 'Sage' stage. Another way to look at it is to think that maybe your own internal world and thoughts are reaching out into the external world of other things. In other words, your internal thoughts are starting to become one with the fabric of external time-space events."

"Wow. I wish I'd known this when I was young, poor, and single. If this is what happens when you stop drinking, I wonder what happens when you give up McDonald's. How come you're into this stuff?" I asked.

"I've had a lot of time to read and absorb a new way of thinking, Tim."

"I'm all for that, and I'll join you as soon as I find the ornament."

When the service is over, we stand in the reception line and Matthew introduces me to the minister.

"Father Emmett," he says, "this is my friend, Tim Allen."

"Pleasure to meet you, Mr. Allen. Glad you could come. I enjoy your show. The one where Tim Taylor is tempted by another woman while playing billiards was a favorite, and figured into my sermon the following Sunday."

"Oh, you mean on 'Thou shalt not commit adultery'?"

"No. On how a man can be eccentric, blow up everything, mystify his wife and kids, and still be a good, trustworthy person."

"Thanks, Father. I liked today's sermon, too." (Oh God. Lying to a priest. Will God strike me dead in his own house or wait until I get into a clearing and away from innocent bystanders?) "I've been away from church for a long time and I think you convinced me to start going again and bring my family."

"Wonderful."

"I hope we see you next Sunday. Good afternoon," he says.

I don't say anything to Matthew as we walk to his car. And then I can't think of much to say except, "Very interesting. Thanks for bringing me."

"Good. What now?" Matthew says.

"I know. Let's go get drunk."

"Exactly what I was thinking," he says with a chuckle. "Seriously, Tim. What now? I'm not talking about what next today, I mean what now in your life."

"What do you mean?"

"A lot of us are real concerned about you."

"What do you mean, a lot of us? What are you talking about? Who is 'us'?"

"You know."

"I don't know."

"You do."

"I don't."

"You do."

"Wait," I say. "You're not homeless, are you?"

Matthews smiles a very knowing smile. "No, I'm not him."

"But you know about him."

"I'm also concerned for you, Tim."

"Well, you're scaring me," I say. "Is this why you called me? Are you *really* Matthew?"

"Yes, of course."

"Why *did* you call me?"

"Because I've been having dreams about you."

"Easy, now. If you're really Matthew, you're still with Peggy, right?"

"Yes, I'm still with Peggy."

"Okay. I'll play along. What kind of dreams?"

"Dreams that tell me you think you're in some kind of distress lately."

"Well, this weekend . . . "

"Right now, things are troubling you."

"What's troubling me is you talking like this."

"I understand."

"You come out of nowhere, in the middle of a weekend that would be weird enough without this, and start telling me about how I'm feeling. And what's worse is . . . you're right."

It bothers me that he's so on-target.

"I'm here to tell you not to worry. You think you're in trouble. But actually you're fine. You're a good man. A positive force. Your instincts are great. It's like driving someplace at night. All you can see is what's in the headlights, but you're still on the road. You're not lost."

"Then how come I keep looking over my shoulder for Rod Serling?"

And how come I'm talking about this with a guy I haven't seen in years who is acting way too familiar with my life?

"Transitions feel that way, Tim. We all go through them. Only our degree of awareness varies."

"You're not TAO/MAN, are you?"

"Who?"

"Just asking."

"Look, you're doing the right thing. You need to answer some questions about life. You're ready for a new phase. It's really kind of exciting, isn't it? You've been opened up to a whole new universe of thought and interaction. You think you're confused, but it's a transition — I know you hate transitions, but isn't that what all of life is? You read, write, look for ways to be a better man. You're a good family man, husband, son, employer, for God's sake. You feel like you're in the middle of the whirlpool, and that seems like trouble and distress, but there are many around you, particularly those with a special insight, who see what you're doing as very positive and centered."

"Great. Is it possible to get that little speech on tape for my answering machine?"

"Did I mention that you're also a funny guy?"

"Yeah, thanks for coming. Try the veal. I'm here all week."

"You're just on a quest, Tim. This isn't your last stop."

"Okay, stop already. This is getting too weird."

"It will be okay."

Suddenly I have a horrible thought. "Wait. This doesn't mean I'm going . . . does it? I mean, you're not the . . . an . . . the angel . . . "

He gives me his broadest grin. "You are a strange man, Tim."

"Then why do you know all this about me?"

"Just an old friend, Tim. Just an old friend. Hang in there. You have the answers. I'll call you again. We'll go bowling."

"Matthew never liked to bowl."

"He does now. Time passes, things change."

We shake hands, Matthews gets in his car and drives away.

*

I'VE GOT A LOT to think about on the drive home. One thing is the whole subject of having the answers. It brings to mind something that happened to me a few years ago when I played at a comedy club in Salt Lake City. I didn't have anything to do during the day, so I figured that while I had some free time I might as well go see the Mormon Tabernacle. The choir sings there and it's supposed to be wonderful. At the time I didn't know much about the Mormons, or the Church of the Latter-day Saints, only that they were another offshoot of Christianity. I thought it was like Protestants or Baptists or Jehovah's Witnesses or Unitarians. I had no idea that they had so much history.

When you get to the big church they take you on a tour through the grounds and buildings. There's even a museum with historical dioramas, like in New York's Museum of Natural History; only instead of a cave family around the fire with the pet woolly mamoth, and a saber tooth tiger lurking in the distance, waiting for everyone to crash, the Mormon dioramas are pretty much a history of their religion. There are replicas of saints and religious scenes behind the glass. I liked the ones with houses and stuff better, because the ones with people look like they're mummified. They're really frightening, actually.

So, I'm on this tour and all of a sudden I think I hear someone say that after his resurrection, Jesus came over to America with a bunch of guys — I think they hit where New York is now, or maybe a little further south — and did some ministering. Apparently he was here for quite a while. Now, I hope I don't have this wrong — I was a little shaken up by the uncanny resemblance between someone on the tour and one of the stuffed saints — but it struck me that Jesus coming to America before Columbus and Eric the Red would be big news to everyone. I certainly had *never* heard of it. I was so blown away that when the group took a bathroom break, I motioned to the guide and said, "No disrespect intended, but this is big news that Jesus came here. *I* didn't know this. Excuse me, but for crying out loud, have you people *told* anybody about this? This is amazing."

He just looked at me sort of funny and said, "The men's room is at the end of the hall."

The group kept moving through the building and pretty soon the guide started in on the story of how a guy named Joseph Smith founded the religion. He began with a little background. Apparently, the Book of Mormon was written by a prophet-historian guy named Mormon (stands to reason), based on the stuff written by other prophets who got their material from prophecy and revelation and put it all down on gold plates. Imagine a very fancy dinner service for the Queen of England, and you'll get the picture. Anyway, Mormon puts all this stuff together and gives everything to his son, Moroni (he's now the angel Moroni, enshrined in gold atop all Mormon churches), who added some of his thoughts and hid the plates in a hill called Cumorah. According to the Latter-day Saints, on September 21, 1823, the same Moroni, now glorified and resurrected, appeared to the soon-to-be prophet Joseph Smith, in upstate New York, and told him about the writings and the plates and how they had to be translated into English.

Said the guide: "Moroni said the proof will be that there's a big tree and if you dig down there will be gold plates that will explain all this." Well, just like Moroni predicted, Joseph Smith found these gold plates, showed them to his wife, showed them to eleven other witnesses who signed statements that they'd seen the goods, changed his life, translated the text into the English language version of the Book of Mormon, and told everyone to move to Salt Lake City.

Right then we turned a corner and smack in front of us I saw a bronze showcase. It was gilded. Ornate. And lo, under the plexiglass cover were 12 gold plates with writing all over them.

I almost fell down.

One minute I was acting irreverent about Jesus's trip to New York, and the next I was face to face with God's dinnerware. Twelve gold plates. I could see by my reflection that my mouth was hanging open. The proof was right in front of me.

I went, "This is unbelievable. No wonder there are so many Mormons." I looked at the guide again. He took a step backwards. I said, "Does anybody know these are here?" He just shrugged and started whispering into his walkie talkie about a troublemaker. Before the security guards could arrive I went directly to the curator's office. I introduced myself and said, "I've just seen the plates. This is amazing. This should be on *60 Minutes*. All they have to do is come see this."

What he said shocked me to the core. "Well, these aren't the *actual* gold plates."

"Wait a minute," I said. "I understand. The real ones are hidden somewhere in the church. These are just for display."

He shook his head. "Actually, Joseph Smith misplaced the real gold plates."

"Boy, you'd think he'd put those in a safe place," I said. "Let's go back to the day an angel gives you 12 solid gold plates. And then what? Give me a break, a week later . . . 'Honey? Those gold plates? I left them in a box after we moved from New York, but I can't find them now. Have you seen them?'

'No.'

'Did we store them in the fruit cellar?'

'No. I didn't touch your stuff.'

'Well, I certainly didn't move them. I'd remember if I had. They're pretty heavy. It must have been you.'

'With all the washing and cleaning and cooking I do all day long, do you think I have time to get into your stuff?'

'What about my other wives? Can you check with them? Number 15 has been acting a little suspicious lately.'

'No one's touched your stuff. Calm down. They're around here somewhere. Anyway, dinner's almost ready.'

'What are we having?'

'Goat steak and leeks.'

'Again?!'

'Since when don't you like goat steak and leeks?'

'I don't know. . . . maybe since you LOST THE WORD OF GOD!'"

Talk about losing something. If I have to know for certain where something is, I put it in a safety deposit box: stocks, heirlooms from my grandfather. If I had an actual golden service for 12, from God, I might at least put them on the mantle, under the bed, or next to my People's Choice awards. I'm sure Joseph Smith was a wonderful guy, and he did a great job of bringing everybody to Salt Lake City, but wasn't he just a little irresponsible? Maybe that's why they named the university after Brigham Young instead.

*

O F   C O U R S E , you don't have to have the actual plates around to believe in something. That's called faith. That's what religion is all about: believing the divine on faith.

In fact, everyone has a different idea about who God is, or even if God is a "who." I was raised with the traditional Judeo-Christian image of an older man, perhaps 55 or 60, with flowing robes and a white beard. But the older I get and the more I've read about the subject, the more I realize that thinking about God isn't easy since more or less everyone agrees that God is beyond thought and words.

Yet many of us define and experience our personal existence through the Creator and our image of him. (I use the term "Him" not to suggest that God is male, but because it is tradition, and referring to God as "He/She/It" every time is not only a level of political correctness that makes me want to puke, but it's a pain to read and will put this book over the word limit.) Images make it easier to conceive of and have a relationship with God because images are a lot more powerful than abstract concepts. For example, the picture of the gigantic mushroom cloud produced by an atomic explosion compared to the concept expressed in the equation $E=mc^2$. Which has more impact: a big E, some small letters, and a measly number two, or a blast that will leave a very big hole where your city used to be?

The East and the West seem to have very different images and ideas about the nature of God and our relationship to Him.

The East, particularly the Hindus and the Buddhists, say that everything in the universe, including the human race, is God. The

Hindus say that we are God in disguise and that the material world, including our physical bodies, are part of an illusion called Maya that God created for his own pleasure.

Now, the definition of an activity done just for pleasure is "a game or sport." So it appears as if God is playing a game of hide-and-seek with himself.

By the way, this Maya illusion is a really good one: good enough for God to temporarily forget that he's really everything pretending to be everything else. (If he knew, the game wouldn't be any fun.) On our level of existence this illusion seems completely real, and that's exactly what God wants. God disguised as a lion will take a big bite out of God disguised as your butt. And it will hurt. He plays this hide-and-seek game to literally experience everything in existence, and in some mysterious way his experiencing the universe creates it. Don't ask me why he wants to be a human who has just dropped an engine block on his foot, or a jelly fish, or a butterfly, or an oak tree either. God only knows—the fully conscious one, that is; certainly not the one purposely experiencing amnesia in the illusion of Maya disguised as Tim Allen.

Which, without a hint of quantum physics, once again means that "I" may not really be here.

So we're God playing a game. But every game has a point. In hide-and-go-seek the point is to find everyone. That's why the Buddhists say that the whole idea of this existence game is to wake up, to regain consciousness, so to speak, and realize that you are God. They call this Bodhi, which means awakening. Quantum physics is starting to sound a lot like Eastern religion in that the concepts of matter, time, and space are looking more like illusions in our mind rather than solid external reality. Quantum physicists are still messing with the apparent parts of the whole — because that's what God disguised as physicists does — only to gradually discover that the parts, including them, are an illusion and the whole is all there is.

In the Western — Hebrew and Christian — view, the universe is an artifact, a thing created by God. This of course includes us as "creatures" made by God. This also makes us very separate from God our maker. To extend the metaphor, it explains why Lee Iacocca is not a Ford, Ernest and Julio Gallo are not bottles of wine, and Calvin Klein is not a pair of underwear . . . or is he? A Buddhist might experience "Bodhi" and realize that he's God, but we in the West eventually get to *meet our maker*.

"Hi, nice to meet you. Thanks for the arms and legs and the stomach and a special thanks for Big Jim and the twins."

Alan Watts says that one of the major values of Christianity is the "eternal importance of differences" because Christians feel you need differences to experience love and relationships. Why? Do they mean that if you love yourself it's too easy; that it's not a true love; that accepting differences is the only true test? Why are we always being tested? Whose idea was this? I'd like to see him in my office right away.

However, even though Christianity emphasizes differences between God and man, good and evil, etc., it also says God is everywhere. So why go to a church to worship God? A church is man made. God never said, "And let there be aluminum siding." Climbing a tree to talk to God sounds like a better idea since only God can make a tree. And if that tree's on a golf course, all the better. In other words, it's not the place but the mind-set, the focus on spirit that's the most important. Like in physics, if you set up your experiment to create a certain perspective, you get a neutrino. In church, ideally, through ritual you create a perspective or mind-set to get in touch with spirit.

The basic way the West sees God is as a creator and king, separate from his creation and subjects. When you consider the kinds of things that men do to other men — for example, Attila the Hun once had the ears cut off 20,000 people because he had a bad hair day — this image of God as an infinitely powerful human ruler is really scary. If you broke an earthly potentate's laws, the punishment for almost any infraction was death in an entertaining way: boiling in oil, crucifixion, burning at the stake, and my favorite, being fed to the lions. Today we have the tabloids. Lesser punishment usually meant cutting off body parts that you really depend on. I don't think that's changed. Now, just imagine what an angry God would do. You'd not only die but suffer eternally afterwards. No wonder they invented the term, "God-fearing man."

The East maintains that *we* are God and that by certain practices, such as meditation, we can start to become aware of this. As for breaking laws and being punished, they have something called "karma," which simply put means, "what goes around comes around." Buddha said, "You don't get punished for your sins; you get punished by your sins."

Actually, according to the Dead Sea Scrolls, discovered in 1948 in a cave in Palestine, Christ was a member of the Essene brotherhood, which believed in reincarnation and was very Eastern in nature. Jesus said, "The kingdom of heaven lies within." Buddha said, "Look within." And the Hindus say, "Look within, in silence." Looking inward in silence seems to be a big part of all the world's religions. The East calls it meditation, but the Book of Psalms says, "Be still and know that I am God." And the Sioux Indians say, " . . . the holy silence is God's voice." It sounds like what they're all saying is, "shut up and listen." So I'm gonna try.

*

I T'S A BEAUTIFUL DAY, and the sun bathes the world in its warmth and light. I'm in a good mood again. I feel connected to everything. Maybe I even am everything, who knows? One of my *fans* told me I was everything. I nodded and smiled but was thinking, "For God's sake, get a life!" My head feels dreamy. Maybe Matthew is right: I'm on the verge of seeing something, or experiencing something. I might be just about to slip behind this coarsely constructed reality and know the universe for what it really is. Maybe I'm having my first moments of clarity in a long time. Or on the other hand, maybe I'm on the verge of serious psychosis. Either way, something is happening to me, and I don't want to fight it. I'd be a fool not to see that this whole weekend has been leading me somewhere. And best of all, it didn't cost anything.

Maybe I'd better pull over first. I don't want to see everything turn to its wave form. I can't watch energy pockets whiz by when I should be watching the road. Don't need a repeat of yesterday morning.

I wonder if to stare into the face of God will drive me crazy. (I wonder who would blink first.) But how can I be any crazier than I've been for the past 36 hours? What will happen if I get answers? What will I do with them? Now that I've asked these question, I'm not sure I want the answers. What's even scarier is that I've been told by some odd individuals that I've already got the answers. So maybe I shouldn't tempt the universe. You have to be careful what you wish for. Maybe I'm more afraid of the truth than I am excited about it. Okay, partly I'm excited, partly I'm frightened to death. I've had these wonderful thoughts before, and then they slip over to the bad side and I feel like I'm losing my grip of things. For all I know, I'm just two minutes away from blowing it.

Oh, look at the sun dappling that bus stop bench. There's a young couple waiting. He's holding the baby. It's serene. I don't know them, but this very second I feel so much a part of them and everything.

This reminds me of something from John Travolta's movie, *Phenomenon*. He says they found a whole forest of aspen trees in Colorado that isn't a forest of aspen trees at all. It looks like a forest, but it has a common root system.

It's one tree. It's just one tree.

TEN

WHEN I PULL INTO the driveway I linger in the car. It would be easy to once again just sit in these soft bucket seats and think about synchronicity and angels, but after yesterday morning's episode, I don't want the neighbors to start talking. Besides, it's hot in here and I want to change from this suit into shorts and a t-shirt as soon as possible. Time to open the door and get on with life.

I wonder what I should make of Matthew. He blows in from nowhere and out again and knows too much about me. Too many people lately seem to know more about me than I do. Should I feel reassured or very, very afraid? I'll settle for somewhere in the middle — like optimistically paranoid with a little bit of queasiness thrown in for good measure.

Church was interesting, but once again I came away with more questions than answers.

There are sheets of brightly colored paper scattered in the grass and stuck in the narrow space between my mailbox and the little flag you turn up to tell the postman there are outgoing letters. I wish they'd stop leaving these junk advertising flyers everywhere, just for everyone to throw away. I know it's a job, but where's the satisfaction: the sound the windshield wiper blade makes when it slaps down on the paper?

The door falls open when I grab a bunch of flyers off the mailbox. I guess I forgot to take in the mail on Saturday. Shoved inside is a big bundle of envelopes, magazines — I hope the new *Car and Driver* has arrived — and, oh look!, more junk mail.

What now? Eat lunch, see who wants money from us today, and then get back to my search.

*

I'M ABOUT TO TAKE a bite of my turkey bologna and potato chip sandwich, when I see something moving in the backyard. Since the pets are inside, watching me eat, I'd better check this out.

I see the cause: Louis, Kady's classroom turtle, is wrestling with something in the shade of a large cactus type thing, just outside the kitchen window. As part of the first grade experience the kids get to take Louis home and learn to care for a pet. It's a great program. Now Laura and I know everything there is to know about these lovable amphibians. I don't know how Louis managed to scale the walls of his cardboard box and escape, but he's loose and grappling with . . . an apricot.

Do turtles like fresh fruit?

I put Louis back in his box, then see something laying on the lawn behind the pool. I'd better walk over and check it out, just in case it's a dead animal.

Well . . . what did I expect? I am standing over what appears to be a whole bunch of apricots arranged to look an awful lot like — what else? — the hood ornament. If I were Robbie the Robot in *Forbidden Planet*, sparks would shoot around inside my overloaded dome. To say I'm amazed is a vast understatement. I'm as stunned as the first caveman to see an eclipse. I'm talking about a huge, primal wow. On the other hand, in light of this weekend, I suppose I would be disappointed if it the apricots were just shaped like a family crest or something.

But one apricot is missing. Does that mean Louis *took* it, or was the little shit rolling the last one into place? Either way, what nerve. In all the time I have spent with Louis — or is it Louise? — he or she has never before exhibited any geometric design ability. I'm amazed that the thing got out of the box and as far as the giant cactus in the first place. Must have started last week. Maybe I should have a little chat with Kady's first grade teacher about Louis and his penchant for freaking out people he stays with.

But what if Louis isn't responsible for this shocking phenomenon? Then who is? Maybe the crazy farmers who make crop circles do apricots as a hobby. It could have been the goal-oriented FedEx guy doing his bit to help blow my mind. Perhaps one of the homeless guys is using my yard as a crash pad. Maybe he had a little insomnia and decided to try his hand a fruit arrangement to bore himself back to sleep. But none of that tells me the important answer: why? This is crazy.

Maybe *I'm* crazy.

And here's the really incredibly bizarre part: I just realized we don't have an apricot tree.

*

I'M TOO AFRAID NOW to eat. I'd better sit in my office where it's safe. This is no fun anymore. In fact, it really bugs me. After all that's happened this weekend, I still have no clue *why* or how it's happening. I've *seen* enough magic. Now I want to know how the trick works. How much of this crap can anyone take?

What would be nice is if some of the wonderful scientific

discoveries I've been reading about would help, but I don't recall any theory of the universe referring to auto parts or fuzzy fruit. Maybe the answer is metaphysical. If we're really all part of the same thing, then my aura ought to be able to contact the hood ornament's aura and set up a lunch. Instead, I think my only recourse now is to visit the local new age bookstore and see if they're still having that sale on dowsers.

Once again, I'm stuck with more questions than answers. Instead of reconnecting me to real life, everything that's been keeping me up at night has increased my wonderment level. I feel like Dorothy in *The Wizard of Oz*.

I don't know what I expected: Ten Quick Steps to The Secrets of Everything?

I've had deep tangential thoughts about the nature of reality. I've let myself get starry-eyed over the magical concepts of science. Instead of grounding me, this whole personal exploration has pulled my notions of reality out by the roots.

No wonder Laura is begging me to start a good novel.

Maybe Matthew and TAO/MAN are right: I'm headed somewhere. I can't think of any other reason why I feel like I'm stranded on a side road with my thumb out, wearing a silly grin and holding a sign that reads: "Here."

The only bright side is that I've spent a lot of time this weekend thinking about me. This has me worried because I've discovered that the "me" I'm thinking about now is not the same me who started on this little journey of exploration. So I have changed. I'm changing right now. I hate transitions. How come I didn't think about this before I started?

I don't know what to do.

I need help.

*

THERE'S A PICTURE of my dad on my office bookcase. I haven't looked at it closely for a long time. He looked a lot like me; actually, vice versa. If he was alive now I know he would help me through this confusion — or hit me on the side of my head and tell me to snap out of it and finish the lawn. I don't mean that my stepdad wouldn't be concerned. Bill's been by my side in extraordinarily trying circumstances, and I love him very much for it. I guess I'm still responding to the frustration of an incomplete relationship with my real dad.

In fact, staring at his picture now, I realize that it's been really tough handling these feelings all my life. I'm angry that he was taken. Losing my dad traumatized me to my core. It ripped me from the security of the nest. It left me out in the open going, "Wow, this is a big badass world. What am I going to do?"

I've never told this to anyone, but right after my father died, when I was eleven years old, I had a conversation with the Devil. Having been raised a good Christian, I had at the time a black and white, ultimate good/ultimate evil view of the world. I judged what had happened to me with the limited tools I had. I believed the Devil was responsible for my dad's death. And worse. I was also convinced that the Devil wanted to kill me. Not literally, of course. Emotionally.

When I realized this, I was in my room, lying in bed. Without even thinking I challenged the Devil and said, "Yeah, well, fuck you. Take my dad? Fuck you. My dad will always be with me. Fuck you for the pain you've caused me. Fuck you, you'll never get me. Fuck you for your hatred."

Strong words for a kid, but I knew them and if any situation demanded their use, that was it. Those words were my only way to defend myself against the evil I saw in the world. If I didn't fight back then, I knew the Devil would win and what was left of my life would be over. Later, I discovered that those harsh words were also, in a deeply secret place, my way of drowning out a little voice that said I was responsible for my father's death; like had I been there with him that day, or talked a few minutes longer at breakfast that morning, the day's timing would have been thrown off a bit, and the poor bastard in the car behind him would have caught it. So all along I felt something was wrong with me and I was being punished.

Even the worst pain fades with time. But the little voice inside didn't. Although I have always been both on the surface and in my heart a good, caring, fun-loving guy, there's a layer of doubt in between. Trust comes hard. I am always on alert and suspicious. And when the pain of my dad's death resurfaces, with the thought that I am somehow responsible, I can be very difficult to be around.

The weird thing is that this never-ending battle made me strong. Eventually, it gave me the tools to succeed beyond my wildest dreams. It reinforced my will, lent a sense of purpose, and gave me the drive to live. No one would destroy me.

So I had to do it on my own. As a young man, I drifted without goals and eventually "killed" myself by ending up in jail. There, I no longer had a name, only a number. All that had made me who I was, was at that moment taken away. I shared a tiny cell with my anger, pain, and ego, and my world crumbled.

Sometimes trauma is the only way to get healthy. In prison I applied myself, tried to figure out why I'd fallen, and finally realized I was not angry at the Devil, but at God. After all, if God is everything, the Devil is part of him, one of God's creations. By letting my father die, God had let me down. I judged God and found him wanting. God was bad. But how could he be bad? Wasn't God good? And who was I to judge God? I should be ashamed for judging God. Was I in jail for having the nerve to judge God?

This hurt me because I so badly wanted to do good.

If I could have seen into the future, I would have realized that one day I *would* do good. And I might have wondered, as I sometimes still do, if any of this life would have happened to me if my father had lived. Maybe he had to die to set me on my course. Maybe that was his contribution and God's way of arranging things.

This is not an easy idea to get used to. I now love my life the way God arranged it, but I can't get past the feeling that my life wouldn't be my life if my dad hadn't been killed.

In jail I realized I had to change myself. Instead of being angry at God, I had to ask for his help. One day I sat in the darkness and asked God, "Tell me why my father died."

God gave me an answer. A weird answer that I didn't really totally comprehend until I started reading about physics and spirituality years later, but it was an answer nonetheless. And I sort of understood.

He sent me a vision of a salami. I kid you not. On earth we see our days as slices off the salami. But God looks at the salami end-on. He sees a circle. Our lives are all one thing to him, contained within the circle. We live and we die, but it's not like beginning and ending. Our beginning, middle, and end are all part of the circle. There's no sadness, there's no loss of life. We never actually go anywhere.

Of course, it doesn't look that way from our normal, everyday point of view because we add a lot of cheese to it, as well as onions, lettuce, tomato, and a long Hoagie roll. We won't have God's perspective until we've woken up to ourselves being with God and rejoin him. I guess peace comes from getting as much of that perspective as we can while we're still here on Earth.

When I got out of jail, I was a changed person in many ways, but I still had to forgive the man who killed my dad. Of course, evolving is a slow process. I had no intention of doing any such thing.

Then, one night, I took a cab ride with a comedian friend in Washington, D.C. He was an off-white, almost burnt-cream man whose father had been murdered in front of him by four peach-colored men. We were in the middle of a conversation about another comic's routine when the cabbie turned around quickly to face us and said, "What's all the pain back there?" My friend told the cabbie what he could do with his talk about pain.

Moments like this are so rare that even Mr. Mouth listened.

"I'm just saying that you should forgive the guy who killed your father," said the cabbie.

"The hell with forgiveness," said my friend.

The cabbie persisted. "All I'm saying is forgive him."

I tried to interrupt, but the driver cut me off. "Say the words!"

My friend finally gave in. "Okay. I forgive the guy who killed my father." Then he took a deep breath and said, "Jesus Christ, I *do* forgive him. I'm better than this."

We got out a couple minutes later.

Now here's the weird part. On the way back, we hailed a cab and it was the same driver. I swear. He said, "Tim! Remember the guy who killed *your* father?" I didn't remember saying anything about that during the previous ride.

I said, "Yeah, but I'm over him."

"So you've forgiven him?"

"No," I said. "I want to kill him. He killed my *whole* family that night. He regressed us 15 years."

"Say the words."

"*You* say them. I don't . . . have them in me."

"Tell me something," the cabbie asked, "Why, when you talk, is everything about 'me'? Why is it always about Tim?"

That stopped me cold.

"Say the words," he said. " 'I forgive the guy who killed my father.' "

"Okay: 'I forgive the guy who killed my father.' "

And something whooshed right out of me. I felt different. After we reached our destination I looked at my friend and said, "Did that happen?"

"It happened."

I went into the hotel and called everyone in my family. My

younger brother said, "Thank God. We have been going backwards, hating. The guy that hit dad was a drunk and he will have to live with what he did for the rest of his life."

And I will always really miss my dad.

*

I'M TIRED. It's probably a sign of how much pressure I've been under. It's not just this peculiar weekend. I've been a bundle of nerves. I need to find some peace of mind. I'm not happy.

Just last week someone I work with looked at me, shook her head, and said, "What's the matter with you?"

I said, "You know when you're juggling and you drop one ball? Unless you're really good — and considering all the situations I juggle, I'm good — it shakes your confidence. That one ball is down there on the ground. It's rolling around and maybe rolling away, and you've *got to* get it back. The show must go on. You've got to bend down and pick it up, but there's a risk: You might drop them all. I've never dropped one before, but there's always a first time."

She said, "Gee, Tim, I was just talking about the bags under your eyes. Maybe you should try a mud facial and sheep collagen injections."

Right.

*

I'M NOT HUNGRY ANYWAY. It's so nice outside I think I'll take a quick nap by the pool. This chaise is very comfortable. I could easily fall asleep here and never wake up. But I'm in no hurry to fade away, even though it's taken me quite a few years and a lot of soul searching to realize that what God said to me in prison was right. There's no death here. We don't understand death for what it really is. We only understand it from the point of view of those left behind to feel the pain and absence. We have no idea what lies beyond until we get there. And if, when we get to the great beyond, we discover that we really are just God hiding from himself, talk about a surprise party!

Yet no matter how one conceives of death, who could be entirely comfortable contemplating it? No matter how I rationalize it, the realization that I'm not going to live forever bothers me. Unfortunately, the more I think about death, the more I realize there's not a damn thing I can do about it — no matter how much I worry.

These kind of thoughts can really pull the rug out from under you. We are all going to die. Period. Life may be full of wonders, but one day it's over. It's a good thing I'm laying down.

I guess one reason people depend so much on religion is that they expect it to give some sort of credence and meaning to death. Well, there is no goddamn meaning to death. Not that it's necessarily a bad thing. Alan Watts, who died in 1973, explains some of this in a lecture called "Death and Rebirth." He talks about death in terms of perspective.

"If we do a speeded-up version of human existence then the problem of death will only be the same problem as the problem of interval . . . It is simply a question of from what point of view you're looking at it.

"Therefore let us imagine a speeded-up movie of human lives, going colossally fast, so that you see people whizzing around . . . But when you get used to it, this will be a kind of natural rhythm like a musical performance. You will see all these shapes and funny manifestations of forms, with arms and legs and heads and so on . . . When you've got used to it, you will see them appearing and disappearing. Another way to look at it is to imagine gazing into a fireplace. The fire is burning and on the soot in the back of the fireplace little sparks keep appearing and disappearing. If you did a speeded-up movie of the universe, you would see the stars going out and coming in.

"In the speeded-up movie of human life — using the familiar technique of time-lapse photography — people would just appear and disappear. And we would begin to detect the recurrence of certain patterns. They would seem to us to form a substantial chain in just the same way as the galaxy, seen from a sufficiently far distance, forms a substantial entity. Therefore we would say when we perceived such a continuous chain, 'That is the same being reincarnated.'"

Then, out of nowhere, Watts blew my mind.

"There you have the full explanation of reincarnation. You don't need any other information whatsoever. You need no spookery, no peculiar initiates, no funny psychic knowledge, no mediums, no nuttin'. All that might add, possibly, to our understanding of it, but the point is that to understand reincarnation all you need is the common knowledge that when you alter the level of magnification, either with respect to space or with respect to time, you see events which you didn't otherwise notice."

Watts also says that there's a way to deal with death while we're alive. You can make a stand against death. You have to be willing to live today as if you're *already* dead, as if death no longer has any power over you. He said not to wait until you're old and sick to consider death, but to think of it right now. We're all born to die and the time in between is ours alone. This life, this living, is dying. So realize you're already dead, take your stand on the idea of Nothingness now, and live your remaining days free of the fear of death because that very fear causes most of our bad behavior.

A mid-life crisis can be defined as the ego's sudden awareness of its mortality.

Of course, what he's talking about — while you're still alive — is not an actual death, but the death of your ego.

It's not easy. The ego doesn't want to die. Part of its nature is the desire to retain its form. So the ego screams "Oh my God, I'm not going to be here any more! Besides, I'm so unique and cute, how will the world do without me?"

Even if your ego can be convinced that its demise is for the best, it wants to stick around to witness the joyous transformation. This is a paradox, much like wanting to commit suicide because of too much pain, and somehow expecting to open your eyes when you're dead and feel great relief at having solved the problem.

Can't be done.

*

I'VE ALSO BEEN THINKING about good and evil. When I was young, I believed the two qualities were separate and struggled against each other in a battle only one could win, and would win *completely*. Of course, that's the Western way of looking at it.

The Hindus believe that good and evil are a part of the game of God, called the dance of life, or "lila." When dancing the rumba, you don't worry about why you swing your butt to the left and then swing it to the right. You just swing it to the left so that you can have the fun of swinging it back to the right. The right is not out to beat the left or vice versa.

It's only humans who classify, reduce, define, and deconstruct the whole of life into parts. Only *we* see good and evil as separate and battling. I say let's think of one implying the other, infinitely.

These days I think of good in all its incarnations as *progressive*. Love, charity, hope, and all the rest make life move forward. Fear, violence, hate — they're *regressive*. They retard us. But beware of people who claim to be just one or the other. Love people who are both — and know it. Remember, we're all from the same tree.

I feel like everything is a matter of perspective. You can see things from the perspective of the ego, which is full of good and evil; or you can come from the point of view of the spirit, which is beyond good and evil. This Oriental parable puts this thought in easy-to-understand terms.

There's a man who feels so lucky because a rich man has given him a wonderful white stallion. He feels this is decidedly good. But then his favorite son gets thrown from the horse and breaks his leg. This is decidedly bad. However, a little later on, the king's soldiers come to conscript men to go into the army to fight and die. But the son has a bad leg, so they let him go. This is real good. Good and evil, evil and good. They change with the circumstance. It's part of the dance. Cha cha cha.

We have *both* inside us. However, we can choose which to emphasize in our lives. We can force the scale. We can choose to love. It's really that simple.

If only it were always that easy.

Once I was hanging out with a good buddy of mine named Baba Ram Bindu (Richard, in English), who has studied Eastern religion. I was suffering from P.M.S. (Poor Me Syndrome) and had downed a couple beers, to boot. Finally, this guy got tired of me complaining about good and evil, suffering and pain. He took a quarter out of his pocket and stood it on edge on the table top, holding it in place with the tip of his index finger. He said, "You see the 'heads' side? That's all the bad shitty things in your life — your dad getting killed, the nightmare of prison, and all the suffering you see in the world. Now the 'tails' side is all the good stuff — love, Laura and Kady, fame and fortune, and all the best stuff in the world—laughter, beauty, joy." Suddenly he gave the coin a flick and it danced across the table in a spinning blur. It looked like a little silver orb slowly waltzing on the table top. He said, "That's the dance of life. That's 'lila.' Notice you can't tell one side from the other. In fact, there are no sides. It's just a little round silver blur. It's one thing. And that's how life is here on the earth plane."

*

I WISH I COULD BE as positive about where this whole search is leading me. All these brilliant guys I read, they get you to the threshold, but they can't make you step through the door. I'd like to, but not many of us do. I know a lot, but trying to make it work for me is tougher than it looks.

I feel like I've hit a brick wall. I am the proverbial buck in the forest who ran as fast as he could, right into a tree. He got dazed, put his head down, and ran into the tree again. He gathered himself, backed up, charged, and ran into the tree again. He kept running into the same tree. All he needed to do was hold his head up and look where he was going, but he didn't. I keep running into the same tree. He was a dumb buck. I'm not.

I explained this to my friend Richard and he said, "I know your problem."

"Yeah? What?" I said.

"You're too interested in the path."

Maybe he's right. I've got my eyes focused on my feet and I'm not looking where I'm going.

"Hey! Look how fast my feet are moving! Whoooeee."

Boom!

"All you've got to do, Tim," said Richard, "is look up and walk around the tree."

But how? What's the equivalent of looking up?

I'm so tired. I'm drifting off. Maybe I'll figure it all out after I wake up.

ELEVEN

OW! I FEEL LIKE I'm on fire. Is this hell? No, it's just Los Angeles. But I forgot to put on my #45 sunscreen before I passed out on the deck chair. Why can't I remember that this was once a desert? Those underground sprinklers can be so darn deceptive. I hope I'm not too badly burned because it will increase my makeup woman's work tenfold, to say nothing of her temper.

I'm dizzy from sleeping in the sun. I need a drink of water. What time is it? 3:15 p.m. I've got to pick up Laura and Kady at 5:30. Guess I've really blown it. No hood ornament. I'll have to apologize to the Celebrity Wheels people in the morning. What a way to start my birthday. Hey . . . it's my birthday tomorrow! I totally forgot. How old will I be? That's something I'd like to forget. Now I'm in an even worse mood.

Here come the pets.

"What do you want?" Silence.

"Forget it. Don't even bother to answer."

I'd better go inside.

This kitchen's a mess. I still haven't opened yesterday's mail. Alright, let's see who wants money. Bills, bills, ads, bills, credit card offer, a very late Christmas card . . . what's this? Wow. It's a letter from my friend Chris Rush. Something tells me I should have expected this, but of course I didn't.

I'm going to sit in the office and read this.

Chris is a brilliant and mystical comedian and writer. He has a shaved head, and he both looks and gives answers like that Magic Eight Ball toy that tells your fortune, only you don't have to shake him. About a year ago, after reading somewhere that I was into physics, he decided to send me *The Dancing Wu Li Masters* by Gary Zukav. The book was about new quantum discoveries and the nature of existence. Had Laura known, the book would definitely have been intercepted. Chris probably thought he was doing me a favor. Instead, he inflated my obsession with searching for the big answers to epic proportions. I think I can safely blame many sleepless nights on Chris. Laura, who has never met the man, feels like he's been living in our guest room for months.

After reading the book, I sent Chris a letter with my reaction and a bunch of questions. I never heard from him again. Now, suddenly, this thick envelope shows up in my mailbox just as I'm going through the greatest reality crisis of my life. Seven months to answer a letter?

Let's see what he has to say.

June 7, 1996
Dear Tim,

I'm sitting in the middle of my living room floor naked, my body covered with physics equations, diagrams and excerpts from obscure Tibetan texts, all drawn in multicolored magic marker. I rock back and forth in a classic autistic manner, while chewing my interdermal nicotine patch. I'd really like to relieve myself now, but even if I could find the bathroom through the floor-to-ceiling maze of physics books and secret Masonic scrolls, I couldn't use the toilet bowl, which I converted into a make-shift cloud-chamber. That dry ice can really hurt your privates. My mind is gone, Tim. There was a loud crackling static-like sound and the smell of ozone and then the image of Porky Pig saying, "tha-tha-that's all, folks."

I was deeply moved by your letter, to the point that I decided that with fifteen years of hobby-level quantum physics under my belt and a couple of years as a molecular biologist, I would attempt to answer your quantum questions and solve these pesky reality riddles. So after collecting the appropriate research materials from my local bookstores and libraries, and using my Mafia connections to acquire those "hard to get" items — that Vatican Museum is a bitch to crack — I scored a gallon of ginseng extract and a special mixture of ginkgo baloba and peyote (the Aztecs gave this stuff to human sacrifice victims, who were known to giggle while having their hearts torn out), to invigorate and hone my mind for the task.

By the way, please excuse me for the ridiculously long time it has taken me to answer your gracious and thoughtful letter. If my apology does not suffice I will make amends in the traditional manner of the Yakuza (Japanese mafia), by cutting off the pinkie finger of my left hand. However, this will slow down my writing speed and may delay future correspondence, and that could lead to a painful and debilitating cycle.

In your letter you exhibited the rarest combination of traits possible in an adult human: high intelligence, subtlety of mind, a sense of wonder, humility, sincerity, a love of knowledge, and big balls. You talked about the kind of stuff that could lead to what Jonas Salk has called meta-biological evolution, which means the evolution of human consciousness, and suggests the survival of the wisest rather than the fittest. You also scared the hell out of me because another amazing aspect of the T.A. letter, as I've come to call it, was its synchronistic arrival at the exact moment I was assessing the mass appeal potential of a one-man show and book about the nature of reality.

However, there seems to be a definite philosophical difference in the direction each of us has taken upon immersion into the quantum realm.

You declare yourself a reductionist. I quote: "The problems began with the concept of superstring theory. I call this, 'that from where all comes.' The path of the reductionist like me is to wonder: What's 'that' composed of?"

To my mind, applying rigid reductionism to quantum exploration is like trying to fuck a smoke ring. In fact, you suggest the futility yourself when you ask, "What are superstrings made of?" We'll get to superstrings in a moment.

There is an obvious advantage in being able to explain complex things in terms of simpler ones, or larger systems in terms of smaller. In fact, the reduction from complexity to simplicity is the essence of scientific analysis. However, its drawbacks become apparent when, as physicist David Peat says, analysis adopts the position of "nothing but." When chemistry is "nothing but" the physics of molecules, an organism is "nothing but" its constituent chemistry, and mind "nothing but" the nerve cells and neurochemicals in action, then a narrowness of perspective results.

By contrast, I believe, matter and mind must be understood through dual, even multiple descriptions, each complementing the other. I agree with Peat when he says, "Qualified reductionism . . . has its place, but when it pretends to offer an exhaustive account of nature, then misrepresentation and confusion result." This universe of Bohr and Heisenberg in which we participate in the creation of our world by the very act of observing it, this fundamental interconnectedness of things suggested by quantum theory and proven by the experimental verification of Bell's nonlocal reality, this Einsteinian relativity of space and time — all point to a very different world view than that of the simple cause-and-effect, clockwork model of Newtonian mechanics. It points through the Looking Glass.

In spite of the important mind-blowing revolutions and paradigm shifts that have taken place within physics, the old ways of thinking continue to dominate our view of reality. Even scientists themselves, who accept what has been called "post-modern physics," retain many of the traditional attitudes of 19th Century science. They look for ultimate primary particles and elemental entities out of which the physical universe is supposed to be built. Many consider consciousness to be an epiphenomenon of the physical brain.

The concept that the brain generates consciousness as a sort of byproduct of its electrochemical thought and sensory processes is strange, since many eminent scientists, such as Nobel Laureate Eugene Wigner and the famous mathematician John Von Neumann, say that consciousness creates everything *including* the brain. John Wheeler of Princeton, who coined the term "black hole," and is one of this century's most respected physicists says, "I do take one hundred per cent seriously that the world is a figment of the imagination." So which came first, the chicken or the egg?

Ironically, many scientists have not yet caught up with the deeper meanings implied by the exploration of their own subject. However, some scientists are intuitively moved by these deeper implications. Inevitably, these are the researchers who move our knowledge of reality forward in a major way. The late Nobel prize–winning physicist David Bohm is such a man, and I really dig what he has to say.

You see, Tim, one of the best-kept secrets of science is that *physicists have lost their grip on reality.*

Thanks Chris, if you would have sent this letter in a more timely fashion, maybe I wouldn't have had to lose "my" mind.

By this I don't mean that they are like a guy who dresses all in red with a white hat and thinks he's a bottle of ketchup. I mean they have no single, solid definition of reality. Knowledge of this reality crisis does not get to the general public because of the mind-numbing mathematical formalism that scientists use to communicate, and the very human tendency of physicists to play up their successes while downplaying their confusion and uncertainties.

Even among themselves, physicists prefer to pass over the troublesome reality issue in favor of "more concrete" questions, like how many quarks can dance on the head of a pin. In fact, there are about eight versions of how the world works according to quantum physics. They're discussed in Nick Herbert's book, *Quantum Reality*, which was originally published in 1985. Since then, several other versions of reality have been added, and before I finish this letter, there may be several more. However, as Herbert says, they all sound "like the tales of mystics and madmen," so full are they of magic and wonder.

So fasten your psychic safety belt.

And reach for the vomit bags. I'm expecting a thrilling but bumpy ride.

Quantum Reality #1 and #2: The Copenhagen Interpretation. Part I (There is no deep reality). Part II (Reality is created by observation). It is Niels Bohr, one of the founding fathers of quantum theory, who first made one of its most outrageous claims that there is no deep reality. He means that the everyday world we see around us is real enough, but it floats on a world that is not as real. In other words, the things and events of our normal world are not made up of normal things and events, but out of an entirely different kind of "thing." This is not a far-out or minority position. "There is no deep reality" is the prevailing doctrine of establishment physics. I think Cornell physicist David Mermin summed up the weirdness of all of this when he said, "We now know that the moon is demonstratively not there when nobody looks." If you ask me — and you did — this is a good place for some Halloween sound effects.

Quantum Reality #3 (Reality is an undivided wholeness). This one reeks of Oriental mysticism, and yet one of its main proponents is Walter Heitler, author of one of the big-time standard text books on the light/matter interaction. Heitler accepts that an observer created reality, but adds that the act of observation also dissolves the boundaries between observer and observed. "The observer appears as a necessary part of the whole structure, and in his full capacity as a conscious being. Object and subject have become inseparable."

Great, I see, therefore I am?

Quantum Reality #4: The Many Worlds Interpretation

(Reality consists of a steadily increasing number of parallel universes). This one, I think, is the most far out, and yet it has gained considerable support among quantum theorists because it resolves the notorious quantum measurement problem — which is that you can't measure anything. (How can a theory based on probability give definitive and accurate answers?) I kind of like the thought of a universe parallel to ours, but slightly different, so that in it O.J. Simpson is a skinny little blond guy who regularly gets the shit kicked out of him by a 300-pound black woman named Bertha.

Quantum Reality #5: Quantum Logic (The world obeys a nonhuman kind of reason). I'll make this one short and sweet: If we all think like crazy bastards, the craziness of the quantum world will make sense.

Finally: something I understand.

Quantum Reality #6: Neorealism (The world is made of ordinary objects). An ordinary object is an entity which possesses attributes of its own, whether observed or not. This is heresy in the eyes of establishment physics. The main neorealist rebel was Einstein, who said of Heisenberg and Bohr's quantum theory: "[Their] tranquilizing philosophy — or religion — is so delicately contrived that for the time being, it provides a gentle pillow for the true believer from which he cannot very easily be aroused." That's a classy put-down from the Big E. The weird thing is that the small group of neorealist rebels with their primitive notions include many of the founding fathers of quantum theory. Besides Einstein, there's Max Planck, whose discovery of the constant of action sparked the quantum revolution; Erwin Schrodinger, who devised the famous "cat in the box" experiment to illustrate the uncertainty principle; Prince Louis de Broglie, who predicted the wave nature of matter; and more recently my main man, David Bohm. Even this quantum reality, closest to the old-fashioned idea of a "normal" world, contains the fantastic requirement that some objects move faster than light, which entails time travel and reverse causality.

Quantum Reality #7 (Consciousness creates reality). This one is easy to sum up: Physical objects have no attributes if a conscious observer is not watching. As Nick Herbert says, "At the logical core of our most materialistic science we meet, not dead matter, but ourselves." Put another way, this theory supports the idea that a tree makes no sound when it falls in the forest unless there's someone there to hear it.

So when I'm fast asleep, the bed's not really here?

This version also has some very heavy supporters such as the genius world-class mathematician, John Von Neumann. Von Neumann invented the concept of the stored-program computer, which has evolved into both super-computers and the one on your desk. He also worked on early robots and helped develop the atomic bomb. But his biggest contribution to quantum physics was his book, *The Foundation*, which is the mathematical bible of quantum theory. (I don't know what the hell he did on weekends.)

In other words, as physicist Eugene Wigner, Von Neumann's Princeton colleague, said: "It is not possible to formulate the laws of quantum mechanics in a fully consistent way without reference to consciousness. It will remain remarkable in whatever way our future concepts may develop that the very study of the external world led to the conclusion that the content of consciousness is the ultimate reality."

Quantum Reality #8: The Bisected World of Heisenberg (The world consists of potentials and actualities). The key here is the probability wave, which means a tendency for something. (You wondered in your letter to me why you only had a "tendency" to exist.) This notion introduces something *between* the idea of an event and the actual event, a bizarre kind of physical reality where possibility and reality meet. Everything that happens in our world comes out of probabilities set up in the world of quantum potential. The magic act of measurement creates an actuality. There is no deep reality as we know it, only tendencies and urges. This is also known as the Shrinks and Hookers Corollary.

At this point in all this madness, I would like to remind you that *quantum theory is 100% accurate in all cases*. And more amazingly, all of the eight quantum realities are experimentally indistinguishable, and each of these realities predicts *exactly* the same results!

No wonder everything tastes like chicken.

Well, I guess it's time for the superstrings you mentioned in your letter. The name sounds like a Remco Toy. "Hey Kids! From the folks who brought you Crazy Ball, now Super String!" This is the theory of everything. Not only do these strings account for the structure of elementary particles, but they also provide a natural explanation for all the forces and interactions of nature and possibly even for the underlying structure of space-time itself. That's what it says in the best book on superstring theory I've ever read . . .

Hey, what's that ringing noise? Not those wind chimes again. What weird thing is going to happen now? Oh, it's just the phone. Bad timing. I'm too focused. This is why God created answering machines.

. . . which is *Superstrings and the Search for the Theory of Everything*, by F. David Peat. You ask a logical question: What are these magical strings, themselves, made of? In this theory, matter is pictured in terms of quantum strings that have an incredibly short length of 10 to the minus 33rd power, centimeters. This is what scientists call "really itty bitty." It means that if we could imagine shrinking down from our own size to that of a single elementary particle, we would then have to perform an equally powerful act of imagination to shrink down to the size of a superstring. I think the key word here is "picture."

In Greek, the word "idea" means "picture." So that's your answer: *Superstrings are made of an idea.*

I know this answer is probably not satisfying to the "Tool Guy" materialist-reductionist part of the entity called Tim Allen. But please bear with me because we are coming to a critical point where superstring theory (which you call in your letter, "that from where all comes") and my basic theory of choice, Bohm's *implicate order* (which *I* call "that from where all comes"), in a sense may interphase. Oddly enough, we are also approaching a point where our two philosophies *seem* to diverge. Yours is basically materialistic, leaving you, as you put it, "in a world very unconnected to my consciousness." Mine is basically mystical or spiritual, leaving me in a world intimately connected on all levels to my consciousness. (Please note: I use both mystical and spiritual in a scientifically based, non-religious sense.)

Now on to the string thing.

In the good old days, generally speaking, there was no great distance between what could be measured and observed experimentally, and what could be conceptualized and described mathematically in theories. However, things are very different now when advanced theories of physics bear little direct connection with anything that can be measured.

Theories today are really emerging out of *other theories*. And the mathematical language in which these theories are expressed has become so advanced that it is no longer possible to give simple visual illustrations of what theories mean.

However, Peat thinks that "string theory," rather than being just the theory of everything, may ultimately be the door to other universes. This is where string theory seems to interphase with Bohm's Implicate Order Theory.

When Bohm's textbook, *Quantum Theory*, was published in 1951, it was hailed as a classic. But being a true intellectual pioneer, he was already looking for deeper explanations and searching for a better way to describe reality. He did this in another of his books, *Wholeness and the Implicate Order*. He says that everything in the universe is part of a continuum, and that there is an infinite spectrum of orders. One of Bohm's key ideas was the *holographic nature of reality*. Even though you probably know about them, I'll briefly describe holograms. They are laser-generated 3-D pictures produced by interference patterns on regular photographic film. And the amazing thing is that every tiny piece of holographic film contains the whole picture. Bohm says that the tangible reality of our everyday world is really a kind of 3-D illusion. Underlying it is a deeper order of existence, a vast and more primary level of reality that generates the world as we know it, and like a holographic picture, even the tiniest piece of our physical world contains the whole universe.

He calls this deeper level of reality the *implicate* (which means enfolded) order, and he refers to our own level of existence as the *explicate*, or unfolded, order. He got the idea while reflecting on the different degrees of order in nature (this is pre-Chaos theory), and seeing the following glycerin cylinder demonstration on the BBC.

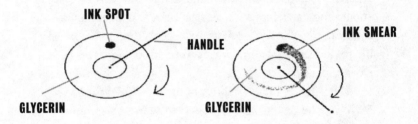

INK SPOT

HANDLE

INK SMEAR

GLYCERIN

GLYCERIN

When a drum of glycerin is turned one way, the dot of ink smears out and eventually disappears, but when the direction is reversed, it reappears. Bohm explains everything in terms of enfolding *into* and unfolding *from* this implicate order. Therefore, to Bohm, an electron is not just one thing, an elementary particle. He believes an electron is an ensemble enfolded throughout the whole of space, and "electron" is *just a name* given to the electron holo-movement's particle aspect. When an instrument detects the presence of a single electron, it is simply because one aspect of the electron's ensemble has unfolded, like the ink drop unfolds out of the glycerin. It also explains the wave/particle nature of a quanta.

According to Bohm, both the wave aspect and particle aspect are *always* enfolded in a quantum ensemble, and it's *the way an observer interacts with the ensemble* that determines which aspects they see unfolded, in much the same way as a jeweler manipulates a gem to determine which of its facets become visible and which do not.

This does not mean that the universe is a giant undifferentiated blob, says Bohm. Things can be part of an undivided whole and still possess their own unique qualities — kind of like individual humans as parts of the human race. To illustrate what he means he points to the little eddies and whirlpools that often form in a river. At first glance such whirlpools appear to be separate things and possess many individual characteristics (as do subatomic particles) such as size, rate, and direction of rotation, etc. But closer scrutiny reveals that it is impossible to determine where any given whirlpool ends and the river begins.

But Tim, Michael Talbot's book, *The Holographic Universe*, leads the way to possibly the most stunning realization of all.

Talbot says that when physicists calculate the minimum amount of energy a wave can possess, they find that every cubic centimeter of empty space *contains more energy than the total energy of all the matter in the known universe*! Some physicists refuse to take this calculation seriously and believe it must somehow be in error. Bohm, however, is certain this infinite ocean of energy exists and that it tells us about the seemingly infinite nature of the implicate order. He feels physicists ignore the existence of this enormous ocean of energy because like fish, who are unaware of the water in which they swim, they are conditioned to focus on objects embedded in the ocean, in other words, on matter. But matter does not exist independently from the sea, from so-called empty space. It is part of space.

To explain what he means Bohm offers the following analogy: A crystal cooled to absolute zero will allow a stream of electrons to pass through it without scattering them. If the temperature is raised, various flaws in the crystal will lose their transparency, so to speak, and begin to scatter electrons. From an electron's point of view, such flaws would appear as pieces of "matter," floating in a sea of nothingness, but this is not really the case. *The nothingness and pieces of matter (whether they're crystal flaws or human beings) do not exist independent from one another. They are both part of the same fabric, the deeper order of the crystal.*

To sum up, in this model of reality, the universe is not separate from this cosmic sea of energy, the universe is a ripple on the surface, a comparatively small "pattern of excitation" in the midst of an unimaginably vast ocean. Says Bohm, "This excitation pattern is relatively autonomous and gives rise to approximately recurrent, stable and separable projections into a three dimensional explicit order of manifestation." In other words, *our reality.*

Ripples on a cosmic sea of energy? I'm beginning to feel seasick.

Bohm also believed that *consciousness itself* is enfolded in this implicate order, and he was way ahead of his time in his idea of "informational waves," which predates I.T., or Informational Theory — which says the smallest basic part of the universe is an info byte. Michio Kaku (who wrote the book, *Hyperspace*) says I.T. is the hottest new thing on the scene, and it is being developed by physicists at IBM and at Los Alamos.

Bohm's got some very heavy guys who support his

ideas, including Nobel Prize winner Brian Josephson, who believes Bohm's implicate order may some day even lead to the inclusion of God and mind within the framework of science.

Tim, this letter is getting too long and my ass hurts from writing it in one long six-day bender. Writing comes hard to me, while talking is my greatest pleasure. So I hope we can meet soon and talk about all this. I originally wanted to add a long section on the awesome topic of the interphase of science and mysticism, which I believe to be the most profound element of this time in human history: but I'm just too burned out. However, I would like to remind you that modern science has its very roots in the mystical realm. Chemistry can be traced back to medieval alchemy and physics grew out of natural and metaphysical philosophy. The renowned nuclear physicist Oppenheimer said: "The general notions about human understanding . . . which are illustrated by discoveries in atomic physics, are not in the nature of things wholly unfamiliar, wholly unheard of, or new . . . What we shall find is an exemplification, an encouragement, and refinement of old wisdom."

The Tantric theory of matter contains the concepts of "nada" and "bindu," which are identical to the concept of matter being both wave and particle, in quantum physics. "Nada" means "movement," or "vibration," and "bindu" means "point." Carlos Castenada, writing about the Mexican Indian sorcerer Don Juan in *Tales of Power*, says, "Don Juan already made the point that there was no world at large but only a description of the world which we had learned to visualize and take for granted." This is almost identical to the physicist Bohr saying: "There is no quantum world, there is only an abstract quantum description." Talbot points out that ancient Hindu literature describes matter as being composed of "anu" or atoms, and says that the subtle vibratory energy of the human energy field exists "paramanu," literally "beyond the atom." Bohm also believes that at a sub-quantum level, or "beyond the atom," there are many subtle energies still unknown to science. Bohm says, "If our attention can go to those levels of subtlety, then we should be able to see more than we ordinarily see."

This seeing beyond the ordinary has been called the mystical experience, and although it transcends logic and language, the mystical experience is very highly regarded by many great rational thinkers, from Niels Bohr, to Heisenberg, to Pythagoras, to Einstein himself, who voiced the opinion that, "The most beautiful emotion we can experience is the mystical. It is the source of all true art and science. He to whom this emotion is a stranger, who can no longer wonder and stand rapt in awe, is as good as dead."

Tim, it seems to me that in the final analysis you can't separate physics from metaphysics. In philosophy, idealists maintain that the essential nature of the universe is spirit; pantheists assert that spirit pervades the universe. This sounds a lot like Bohm's implicate order. The idea that we are a part of this and creatively connected to it through our consciousness makes me a bit "light"-headed, pun intended. The great physicist John Wheeler sums it up when he says: "There may be no such thing as the 'glittering central mechanism of the universe' to be seen behind a glass wall at the end of the trail. Not machinery, but magic, may be the better description of the treasure that is waiting." So I guess it's true: God and magic are everywhere. And everything.

Your friend in awe,
Chris Rush

*

HOLY SHIT! The timing of this letter is incredible. There is so much — almost too much — to think about. I'll probably re-read it ten more times: five times just to grasp it, and five times more just because, like a great movie, I know I'll discover new things each time that I didn't notice before. But right now I feel like a kite that's had its string cut. I love this floating sensation. Even more, I love the sense it makes.

So it's true: Modern physicists have lost *their* grip on reality. I thought it was just me. All those nights of reading so many different ways of saying the same thing would confuse anyone. Just like me, physicists tried to grab the whirlpool, and the *whirlpool disappeared*. They got to the end of the rainbow, and there was another rainbow.

The great thing is that this staring in the face of the creator is really okay. It's nothing to be afraid of. Losing one's grip can be the right thing, because you can't find something new until you let go of the old. This makes me feel a whole lot better about what I've been going through.

I hope I don't forget. I'd tie a string around my mind but the restricted circulation and potential memory loss scares me.

Anyway, I need to focus now. Maybe I should go online, check my mail. I haven't logged on since yesterday, which is rare for me.

The modem whistles and connects.

"Welcome. You've got mail."

Uh, oh.

TWELVE

NO PROBLEM. It's just from Bob at the tool factory. I was afraid it might be another one of those weird messages from TAO/MAN, which would really bring me down. After reading Chris's letter, I'm *still* flying. What I really need now is an afternoon with Stephen Hawking and the Dalai Lama. We could read the letter together and discuss the fine points.

Hmm. I wonder . . . maybe TAO/MAN's online. I shouldn't do this, but I can't resist. A couple clicks on the member locator, and . . .

"TAO/MAN is not currently signed on."

Just as well. I'll peek in on the CAR FORUM, then log off. Looks like there's a conversation already in progress.

HOTROD: Has anyone ever tuned tri-power carburetors here?
WHEELIE: Welcome, Toolman.

VETTEHEAD: All it takes is a screwdriver, Hotrod. :-)

TOOLMAN: What's happening, Wheelie. Get that rod finished yet?

TAO/MAN: Hello, Toolman.

TOOLMAN: Tao/Man? What are you doing here?

TAO/MAN: Waiting for you.

TOOLMAN: How did you know I'd be here?

TAO/MAN: You told me.

TOOLMAN: What? I just searched for you. You weren't online.

HOTROD: Who are you talking to, Toolman?

TOOLMAN: Tao/Man. Can't you see him?

VETTEHEAD: Just us juvenile delinquents here.

TOOLMAN: Tao/Man . . . are you there?

TAO/MAN: Yes. You finally found me.

TOOLMAN: We need to talk. Let's go to a private chat room.

TAO/MAN: That's not necessary. Watch . . .

Hey, he made everyone else disappear!

TOOLMAN: How'd you do that?

TAO/MAN: Can't tell you.

TOOLMAN: This is you, Chris, isn't it.

TAO/MAN: Chris who?

TOOLMAN: Come on. You must be Chris. I just got your letter. What a mind-blower.

TAO/MAN: I didn't send you a letter.

TOOLMAN: Stop yanking my chain.

TAO/MAN: I'm not Chris.

TOOLMAN: How do I know you're telling the truth?

TAO/MAN: Chris doesn't own a computer. He's been computer-phobic since H.A.L. 9000 went berserk in the movie *2001*.

TOOLMAN: That's . . . right.

TAO/MAN: What do you want to talk about?

TOOLMAN: Okay: Who are you?

TAO/MAN: Why does it matter?

TOOLMAN: Because you scare me. Why are you acting so strange? I want to know how come you know so much about me.

TAO/MAN: You should be more interested in who *you* are.

TOOLMAN: Somehow I think you're connected to all the weirdness that's been going on this weekend. The homeless guys, the glowing FedEx man, the hood ornament in the movie and then on the collection plate, Matthew at church, the apricots in my backyard . . .

TAO/MAN: You mean the whole growing cloud of synchronicities. You know what synchronicities are, don't you?

TOOLMAN: Yeah. It's like what my friend Matthew said after church: My thoughts are showing up in the world outside my head. That sounds like magic — which, by the way, also scares me.

TAO/MAN: But it all comes from you. You're on a quest. You're regaining consciousness. These manifestations are just your way of waking yourself up. How can you be frightened of yourself?

TOOLMAN: Easy. But you're right. I'm searching. But I'm not so sure I want the answers.

TAO/MAN: Most men don't.

TOOLMAN: Fine, but that still doesn't tell me who you are.

TAO/MAN: Who do you think I am?

TOOLMAN: I don't know, but I'm sure you have something to do with the missing hood ornament.

TAO/MAN: In a way.

TOOLMAN: Wait. You're the old man who sold it to me.

That's what this is all about. You looked in the collector's catalog and found out it was worth a lot of money. You want the stupid thing back.

TAO/MAN: No. But you're warm. The hood ornament is important.

TOOLMAN: I've been searching for it all weekend.

TAO/MAN: It's sort of like a lure, isn't it?

TOOLMAN: Lure? Like in fish bait?

TAO/MAN: Exactly.

TOOLMAN: And *you're* holding the other end of the rod?

TAO/MAN: No. You are.

TOOLMAN: If that's true, then how do you fit in?

TAO/MAN: Since you asked so nicely: Remember how synchronicities are an external manifestation of thoughts? Well, I'm a manifestation of yours. You are searching for answers to the big questions: Who am I? Why am I? What's it all about? You need help, so you created me.

TOOLMAN: What are you, some sort of guru? I should tell you right now that I'm not a guru sort of guy.

TAO/MAN: Call me a guide. Like the books you've been reading for years.

TOOLMAN: I once thought about getting a Sherpa, but my wife wouldn't let me have one in the house. But how does that explain you?

TAO/MAN: Here in cyberspace, where millivolts of electrical energy create a virtual world, the millivolts in your brain, generated by the deep thoughts of your search, have created me. Think of me like something on the holodeck of the Starship Enterprise. We're just a reflection of each other.

TOOLMAN: But why in a computer?

TAO/MAN: It's the Nineties. A few hundred years ago you'd have been talking to goat entrails.

TOOLMAN: So . . . you're not *really* here.

TAO/MAN: The question is, are you?

TOOLMAN: That's one of *my* big questions.

TAO/MAN: To answer the big questions you have to examine little words like "you," "really," and "here."

TOOLMAN: What do you mean?

TAO/MAN: Who are you talking about when you say "you" or "I"?

TOOLMAN: The guy I see in the mirror. Lovable, good-looking, confused, frightened . . . me!

TAO/MAN: You mean all the lies you tell yourself about who you are, including the big one that you are the thoughts, feelings, conditioned belief systems, and learned identity — your personality — all stuffed into a bag of skin called Tim.

TOOLMAN: I guess. If you say so.

TAO/MAN: That's not you. That's ego. You are not your ego.

TOOLMAN: Then what the hell am I, oh wise computer?

TAO/MAN: You are spirit, you are pure consciousness. That's the answer.

TOOLMAN: Gee. Promise me I won't turn into a ray of light. I don't want my family coming home, hearing tinkling wind chimes, and discovering a pile of ashes and an empty suit on the floor. Also promise me I won't pass out from uncontrollable fright in the next five seconds.

TAO/MAN: You're just afraid of losing who you think you are.

TOOLMAN: What if I discover I no longer care about anything I once thought was important, and just want to stare out a window at a tree, or pass out

flowers at the airport? Or even worse, what if I
discover that I've made a terrible mistake and end
up with some little guy slapping me in the face,
saying, "You stupid idiot, who were you listening to?
Voices on a computer? Welcome to the commune,
and by the way, thanks for all your money."

TAO/MAN: But what if you don't lose who you are, but find
out you're *that* and more?

TOOLMAN: That sounds like a good deal, but how can I do
that trick? Either I'm an ego in a body or I'm Casper
the friendly spirit. Right?

TAO/MAN: Don't go simple on me. First understand there's
no trick, no thing you have to do, except to realize
that this is your true nature. It's like the
wave/particle nature of matter. An electron doesn't
have to *do* anything to be both. It all depends on the
perspective of the observer. It's always a wave, but
when we observe it in a certain way, it appears to be
a particle. Same thing with a human being. You're
always pure spirit and unbounded consciousness.
But when the perspective is changed to one of ego,
everything gets channeled through a certain "point
of view" and bingo, there "you" are!

TOOLMAN: Wait a minute. Hold on a second. Are you
telling me that all I am is a point of view?

TAO/MAN: That's right, but I wouldn't put that down by
saying, "Is that *all* I am." After all, you're one of
God's infinite points of view, and unlike a mushroom
or a fruit bat, you have the ability to realize this and
shift your perspective from ego to spirit.

TOOLMAN: So why don't I just make this shift, pass GO,
collect my incredible bonus, and get back to being
myself and more?

TAO/MAN: You know why.

TOOLMAN: . . . you mean the fear?

TAO/MAN: Yup.

TOOLMAN: Well speaking for my timid ego, it sounds like a valid fear since I believe they refer to this shift of perspective as "ego-death."

TAO/MAN: The ego is always afraid because (A) Deep inside it knows it's an illusion, and (B) It knows it's doomed to extinction when the body dies.

TOOLMAN: Well, spirit sounds like a much better deal, now that you mention it. But you said I could have both.

TAO/MAN: You have no choice. You *are* both. That's what it means to be human. It's just a matter of which one you identify with the most when you reflect on who and what you are.

TOOLMAN: So what am I?

TAO/MAN: Well, as they say nowadays, you are not a human being having an occasional spiritual experience, you are a spiritual creature having an occasional human experience.

TOOLMAN: Really?

TAO/MAN: Good question. The next little word: "really." Which means, "in reality." You must know by now, after reading all those physics books, that reality is a construct of mind. It's like a bottomless pit filled with Jell-O, always wiggling and changing as you go ever deeper into it. Once in a while a consensus of minds freezes the Jell-O, but that consensus inevitably changes and the wiggling starts again.

TOOLMAN: As long as its not lime Jell-O with those weird little orange sections floating in it.

TAO/MAN: Mandarin orange?

TOOLMAN: Yeah, I always hated my Jell-O with fruit

floating in it. Is there anything like that in this reality Jell-O? You know, something solid?

TAO/MAN: There are bits of eternal truth here and there, but they're as different from the mind-constructed reality as the fruit is from the Jell-O.

TOOLMAN: Well, TAO/MAN, you've covered two of the important little words in my big question, "Am I really here?" Should we go for the third word: "here"?

TAO/MAN: Sure thing. But I figure quantum physics has given you big-time clues on this one.

TOOLMAN: I know time is relative and that in physics, past, present, and future are not considered to be in normal linear order; in fact, I've read that physicists and Eastern mystics say that the kind of time that passes, or flows from past to future, is an illusion of the mind. So I guess it took me "no time" to get "here," and how long I stay "here" before I take the time to go from "here" to "there" seems meaningless.

TAO/MAN: That's pretty good.

TOOLMAN: Wait, I'm not finished. Bell's Theorem proves that "here" and "there" are completely connected, and once again the mystics say that time and space are illusions of the mind . . . hey, I am getting pretty good at this. So "here" doesn't seem to make much sense.

TAO/MAN: Right: "Place is to space what time is to eternity." Give that man a cigar!

TOOLMAN: That oughta be a bumper sticker. So, now that I know how it works, what's the point of life? What do I do next? Why am I here? So what?

TAO/MAN: The point of life is to discover our fundamental, unchanging nature.

TOOLMAN: Which is?

TAO/MAN: Happiness.

TOOLMAN: That's it?

TAO/MAN: Isn't that enough?

TOOLMAN: If that's our fundamental nature, then why are there so many unhappy people?

TAO/MAN: Because our society has conditioned us to believe that unhappiness is absolutely necessary.

TOOLMAN: That's ridiculous.

TAO/MAN: No, it's not. It's truth. Take just one small example: Ads sell you things because they convince you that you're unhappy without them. The fundamental nature of man is spirit, right? Spirit is pure, unconditional happiness. Ego tries to attain happiness, but the best it can do is achieve *conditional* happiness through various pleasure producing mechanisms like money, power, sex, or, to give you one close to home, finding the hood ornament. That would make you happy, wouldn't it?

TOOLMAN: Very much so.

TAO/MAN: But that's all fleeting and temporary and contains within it the fear of the happiness disappearing. So how can you ever be happy that way?

TOOLMAN: How about being in my Mercedes with a trunk full of Krugerrands, with the Playmate of the Year in my lap, cryogenically frozen forever in ecstasy?

TAO/MAN: That's a cold way of looking at it. At cryogenic temperatures all motion stops and certain things shrivel and hide. So much for your good times, big guy. Plus, you'd always be afraid of melting — which is just another way of being afraid the happiness would disappear.

TOOLMAN: So, can I ever be happy?

TAO/MAN: Yes.

TOOLMAN: How?

TAO/MAN: By identifying with spirit rather than ego, and enjoying the game of life — played by ego — as a game.

TOOLMAN: And that's it?

TAO/MAN: Yeah. Of course, it's easier said than done.

TOOLMAN: I knew that.

TAO/MAN: Believe it or not, you *did* know that. You've always known that. I told you that you already knew the answers. I told you that you already knew the secret no one was telling you. We're all spirit, and the nature of the spirit is happiness. Happiness is God and that's where we come from. That's what we *are*. Happiness is the way God feels. Choose happiness. Now live it by being enlightened, which by your definition is accepting *what is*. Notice the details of life as they are, and go with them. That's where the saying "God is in the details" comes from.

TOOLMAN: My fingers are really tired. I'd be happy if we were done.

TAO/MAN: You're happy no matter what. It would give you more *pleasure* if you could stop typing.

TOOLMAN: I got it. Bye.

TAO/MAN: Bye.

TOOLMAN: One more thing: *Am* I really here?

TAO/MAN: Yes. No. For the time being. As a human being.

TOOLMAN: Depends on my point of view, right?

TAO/MAN: Right. Bye, Tim.

TOOLMAN: Hey, don't be a stranger. Come over, bring the kids, we'll go swimming, barbecue some steaks, swap wives . . .

TAO/MAN: Cool.

Just as I log off I hear a door slam. It snaps me back to reality. I'd better see what's going on. I walk through the house, and there in the foyer, amidst a pile of knapsacks and carry-alls, are Laura and Kady.

*

"HONEY, YOU'RE . . . " I look at my watch. It's only 5 p.m. " . . . home early."

"Didn't you get my message?" Laura snaps.

"What message?"

"I called two hours ago. A couple of the girls got sick. We had to come home. I left a message for you to pick us up at 4:30. I had to bum a ride home with Shirley Johnson."

"Oh? Is she outside?"

"No. So what happened?"

"Yeah, where were you, Daddy?" asks Kady.

"I don't know. I guess I heard the phone ring a couple hours ago, but I was in the middle of something and then got caught up in something else and never checked the machine. I'm really sorry."

I try to get a little kiss, but both Laura and Kady can only manage tight-pursed lips.

"I'm going to unpack us and get cleaned up. *You* can go back to whatever you were doing that's so important," Laura says.

With that, the girls walk off. Great. Just what I need. A weekend from hell and my wife and kid come home mad. Of course, I suppose when you have a transcendent experience there's eventually only one way you can go: down.

*

I've been in my office for an hour, organizing my books, stacking them on shelves, putting them to rest. I think I've had enough of physics and metaphysics and all the rest for a while. Something tells me I might even get a good night's sleep tonight. That is, if Laura doesn't stay pissed. Then I'll have to sleep on the office couch, and it always messes up my back.

There's a knock at the door. It's Laura. She says, "Can I come in?"

"Sure," I say.

Laura seems like she's in a better mood. I confirm that with a big kiss.

"So how was the trip?" I ask.

"We had a great time," she says. "Kady and I really got to know each other better. She's a great little girl."

"And you're a great mom. Sorry I didn't check the machine."

"That's okay. I'm over it. So what were you doing?"

I'd have to write a book to begin to explain.

"Oh, nothing."

"Don't tell me nothing. You have circles under your eyes. Were you reading again? Did you get any sleep?"

"Some. I'm fine. I missed both of you terribly, but I had a pleasant weekend. I, uh, puttered around the house, watched some movies, went to church . . . "

"Church?"

"Yeah, I got a call from Matthew — remember him? He wanted us to join him. He's sober now. On the program. Church was . . . interesting."

"That must have been nice for you," Laura says. "Did you give Spot her pills?"

"Of course."

"Did you get the cleaning?"

"Yes. Listen, those people are weird. I think they might be from another planet."

"Who cares? They're the only place in town that actually cleans my clothes in an hour. What else did you do?"

"Well, the Celebrity Wheels people called Saturday and they're coming to pick up the hot rod tomorrow. I wanted to install the hood ornament — you know, that one I got in Pasadena — but it seems to have disappeared. To tell you the truth, I've spent most of the weekend looking for it. I don't know what I'm going to do if I can't find it. If you've got any ideas, I could use some help."

Laura's face suddenly falls.

"That little crystal one?" she asks.

"Yeah."

"With the broken base?"

"It wasn't broken. I mean, it wasn't *that* hard to fix."

"You said it was a one-of-a-kind."

"Yeah, I said it was a one-of-a-kind. How did you remember that the base was broken?"

"Did a FedEx come for me?"

"Did you hear what I said?"

"Yeah, about the ornament."

"So?"

"Where's the FedEx?"

"Wait a sec. We were talking about the ornament and how I can't find it, and I just asked for your help."

Laura gives me her familiar "You idiot" look.

"Where's the box, Tim?"

"Why is the FedEx box suddenly so important?"

"Because it's in the box."

"It is not."

"It is."

"Not."

"Why? Did you open it?"

"You know I don't open your stuff."

"Good."

"It can't be in the box. That would mean I've been looking for it all weekend and it's been in my office the entire time."

"That's exactly right."

"Then I *am* an idiot."

"For what?"

"For not looking in the box."

"I thought you said you don't open my stuff?"

"I don't."

"We're going around in circles. Where's the box?"

I reach behind the desk, grab the FedEx box, and hand it to Laura. She hands it right back to me.

"Open it," she says.

"I can't." Suddenly, I am very nervous.

"It's in there. I promise."

"I feel like we're discussing Schrodinger's cat."

"So open the box, collapse the wave function, and create the answer."

Wave function? Laura? "How do you know about that?"

"I have to do something when your snoring keeps me awake. Those books, Tim . . . whew."

So I open the box.

The hood ornament is inside.

"I found Kady playing with it," Laura explains. "I guess she chipped a piece off the base, so I sent it out to Denyon to be restored."

"How'd you know about Denyon?"

"Well, dear, I listen. It's the company that does a lot of antique stuff. They also happened to know what this thing was. It came off some '36 something or other."

"Gee, thanks for clearing that up."

"I was going to give it to you, all fixed up, for your birthday tomorrow. I had no idea Celebrity Wheels would call. Otherwise . . . "

"It's okay," I say, trying to contain my excitement. "Do you mind if I go into the garage and put it on the car now?"

"If it makes you happy," she says, with a little smile.

*

THE RED/PINK RAYS of the setting sun stream through the high garage door windows, casting an almost spiritual aura, as I come in from the house. Spot, possibly sensing my sudden positive mood and an end to a harrowing weekend, tags along.

First, I get the mounting screws and bracket assembly and attach it to the hood.

Now for the big moment.

As I put the ornament in place, I hear music and bells chiming. Where's it coming from? Are angels singing? No, it's the ice cream truck that cruises the neighborhood late each afternoon.

There. It's . . . on. I finally got it installed! Now all I have to do is stand back and admire my handiwork, the realization of a dream. The last bit of sunlight through the windows hits the prismatic crystal base, which bisects the beam into two perfect rainbows. There it is. And it's . . . it's . . .

. . . Wow. *Is that ugly!*

It's awful. It looks like something from a crackerjack box. The whole thing is bigger and more ungainly than I remembered. It doesn't even look like a bird, but more like a flying rodent. And it's *not* made of stone and crystal, but some glass and modalite.

I hate it. It doesn't fit. It's horrible. It doesn't belong on the car. I can't use it. It sticks out like a sore thumb. What could I have been thinking?

I take the ornament off the hood. I can build a better one myself. In fact, I will.

Still, I'm upset. I wasted a whole weekend . . . or did I? My anger fades quickly as I realize that it doesn't really matter since I no longer *need* the ornament to make me happy. And that's the point, isn't it? Ego. Spirit. Waves and particles. As the saying goes, once you've used your finger to point at the moon, and you see the moon — in this case, happiness, and the genuine possibility of more — you no longer need the finger. My life and all my reading were the finger. Happiness is the moon.

And all I have to do is notice the world and accept it the way it "really" is.

With that, I throw the ornament in the trash. Spot walks up and rubs against my leg. I squat down and scratch her behind the ears.

"It was really awful, wasn't it girl? Oh, well, that's the way it is. That's life. Right?"

Spot cocks her head to one side, and looks at me as if she's just come to some sort of critical decision. On her way out, I swear I hear her mumble, in a surprisingly wise voice, "I could have told you that two days ago."

. . . The next thing I know, I hear the whirr of chopper blades in the distance, cutting through the thick and humid morning air. I wipe the sleep from my eyes. It's dawn, the storm has let up, and it's time to go. I toss the tiny tablets with the Answers into my backpack. Also, the priceless jeweled eggs, as a little something for the wife. Then I run across the floating stones, through the pile of bones and brightly colored foil, and out onto the Tepui where the helicopter waits.

I suddenly find myself on a plane heading home to America. I realize that the only decent thing to do is to donate this treasure to the Smithsonian Institute. I want to make the tablets available to all mankind, even if mankind has to stand in line to read them. I figure since we've waited this long to evolve, a couple more hours can't hurt.

Before the man from the Smithsonian comes to pick up the tablets, I invite a few close friends over with whom I can share my amazing discovery. We have a fabulous dinner and wonderful conversation, all in anticipation of the main event. Finally, I suggest they go into the library, while I bring in the tablets containing the Answers. I excuse myself and am halfway across the house, thinking that this is the greatest moment of my life, when I suddenly realize — and I know this is going to sound really, really stupid — that I have completely forgotten where I've put the tablets . . .

SUGGESTED READING

Pirsig, Robert M. *Zen and the Art of Motorcycle Maintenance*. New York: Bantam, 1984.

Capra, Fritjof. *The Tao of Physics*. 3d ed. Boston: Shambhala, 1991.

Kaku, Michio. *Hyperspace*. New York: Doubleday, 1994.

Watts, Alan. *The Book: On the Taboo Against Knowing Who You Are*. New York: Random House, 1989.

and, if you *really* have your shit together:

Hancock, Arthur B., and Kathleen J. Brugger. *The Game of God*. Cartoons by Arthur B. Hancock. Humans Anonymous Press (Box 170045, St. Louis, MO 63117), 1993.